Tiger
by the Tale

CRONOPIO PUBLISHING

1997

Tiger
by the Tale

A CELEBRATION OF TIGER WOODS
GOLF'S NEWEST SUPERSTAR

BY

MARK STEWART

CRONOPIO PUBLISHING

1997

LIBRARY OF CONGRESS CATALOGING-IN-PUBLICATION DATA
Stewart, Mark
  Tiger By the Tale — A Celebration of Tiger Woods, Golf's Newest Superstar
  by Mark Stewart.
  Cronopio Publishing — Norwalk, Connecticut

  ISBN 0–9658048–0–1 (pbk.)

  1. Tiger Woods, 1975 —   , Sports biography.
  2. Men's golf — United States — Biography — Literature.

Library of Congress Catalog Card Number   97–068299

Tiger by the Tale

Table of Contents

Introduction

Had an extra terrestrial visited our celebrity-obsessed planet during April of 1997, he would have dispensed with all that take-me-to-your-leader nonsense and simply made a bee-line for Tiger Woods. And quite understandably so. In the wake of Tiger's stunning victory at the Masters, more words and more attention were focused on him than on anyone in recent memory, including heads of state and bomb-building madmen. It shed some light on who we are as a species, but it also said something important about this amazing young man.

Tiger touched something deep inside people—people who read, people who write, people who think, people who play golf and people who just like to watch sports on TV. For all of the superhuman powers he appears to possess, he seems so very human, and so very good. The airwaves were choked with more and more information about Tiger, some useful, some thoughtful and some not. As a result, and perhaps inevitably, the world began to lose sight of who he is and instead began dreaming of what he could be. Tiger was Jack Nicklaus, Jackie Robinson and Michael Jackson all stuffed into the same golf bag. He fulfilled myriad desires, addressed countless agendas. And, good golly, he was just getting started.

It is a unique burden Tiger Woods must bear, albeit one for which he and his parents insist he has been groomed since birth. Tiger is now officially everything to everyone, and anything anyone wants him to be. This is not a situation that he has sought, nor one he relishes; Tiger is a smart guy, and he knows that trying to live up to such expectations can only lead to bad things. Still, here is a young man, by all accounts a bona fide prodigy, who claims to be immune from the pressure of expectations because none can be as lofty as his own. He may be asking for trouble. Or he may know more about trouble than he is letting on.

A glance at history reveals few 21-year-olds who have risen, even briefly, to the kind of worldwide prominence Tiger enjoys, and even fewer who were prepared to shoulder the mantel of responsibility that comes with it. That, perhaps, is the most intriguing thing about him; not that he has done the impossible—and not even that he planned to do it—but that he was prepared for it when it happened. It almost makes one giddy. This isn't about golf, you see, nor is it about race relations or any of that other stuff. It

is about someone trying to achieve in body, mind and spirit what we all know is possible, but cannot imagine achieving ourselves. We are all on Tiger's team, and we want to win. When he drains a putt, we tingle as if we were the ones reading the break. When he hugs his mom and dad, we are hugging our moms and dads. When Nicklaus gives him a pat on the back, we feel the master's hand on our back. And when he thanks Lee Elder after coming off the 18th green at Augusta, well, we thank him, too. We will even forgive Tiger for his transgressions, if and when they occur, which is saying an awful lot in this day and age.

The smart money says sit back and savor the man, not like a bottle of fine wine, but like an entire wine cellar. Tiger Woods has a lot of years left in him, maybe even beyond his golfing career, and it is anyone's guess when the most exceptional vintage will arrive. It is a little frightening to consider, but right now we may only be sniffing the cork.

Raising a Tiger
The Making of a Golf Prodigy

Nature versus nurture. Golf junkies will debate almost anything, though traditionally this has not ranked among the hot topics among denizens of the 19th hole. But golf tradition itself has been taking a beating lately, thanks to a young man named Eldrick Woods. He has given the game a much-needed nudge, and caused those in-the-know to reassess exactly what it is they do know, and what they still have to learn. Indeed, he has sent the golf world scrambling to answer a very intriguing question: just how does one go about raising a Tiger?

For better or worse, the strange brew of genetics and child-rearing that begat Tiger Woods will, at least for a decade or two, serve as something of a template for the raising of champions. Replicating his upbringing, however, may prove a lot more difficult than people anticipate. Tiger was not your typical, cookie-cutter kid. In fact, there is nothing remotely typical about him.

The strength of spirit that courses through Tiger began to simmer in small-minded midwest America long before he was born, and came to a boil in the steamy jungles of Southeast Asia. The balance and inner peace that define his very being are grounded in a culture more than 20 centuries old. Earl and Kultida Woods came together after starting life half a world apart. Needless to say, their union did not blossom from a meet-cute at the neighborhood malt shop.

Whatever pundit observed that "you only get one chance to make a first impression" could easily have had Earl Woods in his crosshairs when he was first struck by this thought. Despite a calculated stoicism, Tiger's dad, most everyone agrees, is about as subtle as a kick in the groin. But then, developing a sense of subtlety was never on Earl's list of things to do. He was born in Manhattan, Kansas,

> *"My mother always told me I had to be better to get a decent chance, and I found that out to be true."*
> **Earl Woods**

Tiger's golfing prowess has much to do with his multiracial heritage and the unique circumstances of his upbringing.

during the Great Depression and grew up as a target for the kind of racial slurs that could only be hurled at a boy who was half black, one quarter American Indian and one quarter Chinese. When his father died, his mother proclaimed him "man of the family" at the age of 11. It was a symbolic gesture, of course, but he readily assumed that responsibility and all of the pressure that went with it. When Earl's mother passed away two years later, he was the head of the household for real. He has been on edge pretty much ever since.

Earl gained some small measure of relief in sports, where he excelled at an early age. In baseball, he was a good hitter and fielder—far better than most of the white boys who yelled "nigger" when he came to the plate. Not satisfied to simply let his bat and glove do his talking, Earl delighted in putting his intellect into play whenever possible. Once, during a Little League tournament, he responded to a taunt about the color of his skin by challenging his tormentor to compare the undersides of their forearms. Earl's skin was actually lighter. Had he simply spiked the boy, or arranged for a brushback pitch, he would not have made the point he was after.

During the early 1950s, Earl matriculated at Kansas State University, where he became the first black baseball player in what was then called the Big Seven conference. He was a hard-hitting, quick-thinking catcher who was entrusted with handling a pitching staff whose members he was not allowed to room with on road trips. During away games, he usually stayed in black hotels; at white-only restaurants, he ate at the back door while his teammates sat comfortably in the dining room. When he stepped into

> *"I was a black kid, and golf was played at the country club...end of story. But I told myself that somehow my son would get a chance to play golf early in life."*
>
> **Earl Woods**

the batter's box in front of redneck fans in towns like Columbia, Missouri and Ames, Iowa, he heard stuff that made the taunts from his Little League days seem, well, Little League. Off the field, Earl majored in sociology, and minored in psychology—two subjects that would come in handy a couple of decades later.

After school, there was a failed marriage that produced three children. And a military career, where Earl encountered still more racism, albeit with a slightly duller edge. He was a public information officer stationed in Brooklyn, New York, cranking out press releases and occasionally dealing with the media in his own quiet little corner of the Cold War. In his mid-30s, when most men in dead-end Army careers begin looking for opportunities in civilian life, Earl gave his first family the big kiss-off and joined the Green Berets, where he became an explosives expert and achieved the rank of Lieutenant Colonel, distinguishing himself time and again during two tours in Vietnam.

Earl Woods blended military training and a little bit of EST to give young Tiger the mental toughness he would need to compete.

There he fought side by side with Nguyen Phong, a fellow officer in the South Vietnamese Army. Together they stormed through enemy-held villages, sidestepped booby traps, and traversed rice paddies with tracer bullets screaming just inches over their heads. Earl bestowed upon his comrade the nickname "Tiger" for his strength, cunning and iron will. After their brief time together, Phong disappeared, most likely consumed by that dreadful war. To Earl, however, Phong's demise seems unimaginable. To this day, he believes that Phong is alive. He hopes his old buddy will see the names Tiger and Woods in some headline and make the connection.

In 1967, Earl was given a mission that brought him to Thailand. While in Bangkok, he met a pretty 23-year-old name Kultida. Her parents—her father Thai and her mother part European and part Chinese—had separated when she was just five years old, and she was shipped off to boarding school. Tida, as she liked to be called, vowed then that her own child would have nothing but round-the-clock love and attention. Little did she realize that the wild-eyed, dark-skinned Green Beret who sauntered into the U.S. Army headquarters where she worked as a secretary would someday father that child. Nor, for that matter, did she have an inkling of how dramatically her Buddhist beliefs would be put to the test as the Asian wife of a black man in a country that claimed to accept everyone, yet so clearly wanted nothing to do with either of them.

Their first date found Tida and Earl in a Buddhist temple. Their return to the United States two years later as

> "I knew, instinctively knew, Tiger was going to have fame. Some day, my old friend would see it on television and think, that must be Woody's kid, and get in touch. That would make my year."
> **Earl, on Tiger's nicknamesake, Tiger Phong**

husband and wife took them back to Brooklyn, and then to California, where Earl landed a job as a purchasing agent in 1972 with defense contractor McDonnell-Douglas. In 1975, Tida became pregnant, and that fall the family moved into a home in the sleepy suburb of Cypress. Soon, though, the quiet was shattered—as was Tida's kitchen window—during a barrage of limes, rocks, and BBs. A special welcome for the subdivision's first Asian-African-European-American (and, more to the point, non-white) couple.

This event, which took place just weeks before Tiger was born, strengthened Earl's resolve to fashion his own special version of the American Dream. And it intensified Tida's old pledge to make sure her child never knew what it was to face life alone. When her son arrived, on December 30, she dreamed up the name Eldrick—which begins with an E for Earl and ends with a K for Kultida—so he would always know that his parents were at his side. Earl was not exactly thrilled with the name.

Growing up black in America would be hard enough; doing so with a monicker like Eldrick seemed even more unfair. They agreed to call him by the nickname "Tiger."

Ignoring the stares of his neighbors, Earl did his best to settle into life as a white-collar husband and father in Southern California.

Which, of course, meant getting serious about golf. He had learned the game the same way he learned to blow up bridges and ammo dumps in Vietnam: he read a book, practiced his technique, and then went out and got the job done. Earl broke 100 his first time out on a golf course, and by the time he and Tida relocated to Cypress he was a significant cut above most of the hackers who played at the Navy Golf Course, which was just a few minutes from their new home. Hackers or not, the navy men found it unusual to see a black man sharing their course. They called Earl "Sergeant Brown"—a doubly ignorant slur which referred to his skin color and the highest rank

Tiger was already chipping like a pro by the age of 13.

they assumed a black man could achieve. Earl never let on that he outranked his detractors. The club bartender, tired of watching his customers make idiots of themselves, eventually clued them in.

Part of Earl's practice regimen included hitting balls into a net he had rigged up in the garage. The trade-off for this practice time was agreeing to keep an eye on Tiger, who was still an infant when his dad first dragged his high chair into the garage and began slapping five irons into a net. At six months, Tiger began watching Earl swing. At ten months, he climbed down, grabbed a club and began swinging himself. Perfectly. Earl armed Tiger with a sawed-off club and took him to the practice green at the Navy Golf Course and he was holing putts before his first birthday. By 18 months, young Mr. Woods was hitting off the tees at the driving range. And before his third birthday, he was chipping out of the sand, hitting out of the rough, and commenting on flaws in the swings of other golfers. He even played the back nine at NGC and, according to his father, once carded a 48. Tiger hit from the red tees and Earl teed up his fairway shots, but the feat was impressive enough to attract the attention of local sportscaster Jim Hill, who took a crew to capture the prodigy on film. This led to Tiger's storied appearance on *The Mike Douglas Show*, where he made monkeys out of Bob Hope and Jimmy Stewart. Those who have not seen the clip yet need not worry; it will probably be replayed a thousand times over the next two decades.

The other players at NGC were definitely not into the Woods, and they began to raise a real stink when Earl and son actually began playing the whole course together sometime after Tiger's third birthday. Truth be told, this was not exactly Winged Foot or Augusta. There were kids playing the navy course all the time—some under adult supervision and some not. But the sight of Sergeant Brown and his

golfing gnome was too much for some members, and they invoked a little-used club rule banning anyone under the age of 10 from playing the course. A little posturing from Earl got the decision overturned temporarily, but Tiger's privileges were re-revoked soon after. Earl felt that the same members who had given him a hard time when he first began playing were now trying to get at him through his son. He may have been right.

Never one to ignore the rear entrance when the front door was slammed in his face, Earl hit upon a clever idea. When Tiger was four, the club hired a new pro, and Earl approached him with a challenge that sounded so preposterous that he could not risk turning it down. Tiger would

> *"In his own way, he was teaching me initiative. Whether I practiced or played was always my idea."*
> **Tiger**

play the pro 18 holes, with the pro spotting him one stroke per hole. If Tiger won, his playing privileges would be restored. If he lost, Tiger and

Though known for his long driving, Tiger owes much of his success to the creative short iron play he developed on the par-three Heartwell Park course.

Earl would walk away. The pro agreed (how could he not and ever live it down?) and proceeded to choke, losing to a four-year-old by two strokes. Tiger was back in business. Or was he?

The pro was overruled by furious club officials and the ban was reinstated shortly thereafter, so Earl and Tiger started playing at the Heartwell Park Golf Club, a par-three course in Long Beach. The pro there, Rudy Durant, was hesitant to let Tiger play at first. At Earl's insistence, he watched the kid hit a few shots. Not only did Durant let him play, he soon became Tiger's first coach, tutoring him on-and-off for six years. There at Heartwell, on the cramped par-threes, Tiger learned how to use his irons, honed his short game and developed quite an imagination for getting out of tough spots.

Earl, meanwhile, was feeling a lot of pent-up frustration. He could control it, of course—years in the military had taught him how—but he began to sense that it might be adversely affecting his relationship with Tiger. Earl's inclination was to control every second of his son's life, perhaps confusing the role of father with the duties of an officer. He was bright enough to know there was a better way, and he found it through the popular E S T (Erhard Seminars Training) movement of the 1970s. By the time he completed EST, Earl had arrived at some interesting conclusions. He discovered that he could do more good for himself and Tiger if he stepped back and merely provided a lot of support and a little guidance. He became Tiger's best pal, a relationship that continues to this day. Meanwhile, Tida's role suddenly changed. She was still Tiger's mommy, but now it fell on her to do a lot of the hard-core parenting, punishing, and laying down of the law.

Not that Tiger spent much time in time-out. He was kind, obedient and thoughtful. And although he could talk to his parents about anything, he also liked to figure things out for himself. It made Earl and Tida proud, but it also worried them at times. They wondered how much Tiger was

Long before she had Tiger, Tida Woods vowed that her child would receive all of the love and attention she could give.

holding inside, especially after he waited several days before telling them about a terrifying incident on his first day of kindergarten. Some older white boys had grabbed Tiger, tied him to a tree, and threw pebbles at him. And they shouted names like "monkey" and "nigger." It was not that Tiger was afraid to tell his mother and father, he just wanted some time to turn it over in his own mind. His self-awareness took lees troubling forms, of course. At the age of six, Tiger became interested in some subliminal tapes his parents had purchased, and began listening to the positive messages while practicing his swing, putting or watching videos of great golfers. He also taped the sayings to the shelves in his room, and reviewed them every day.

By 1982, the legend of Tiger Woods was beginning to pick up steam. At age six he had already nailed a pair of holes-in-one, and had appeared on several local programs, as well as *That's Incredible!*, one of the highest-rated shows at the time. The kid was even giving out autographs. It is only a matter of time before one of those block-letter jobs turns up on the memorabilia market. And when it does, you can bet there will be a feeding frenzy of collectors getting out their gold coin.

It was also at the age of six that Tiger teed up his first ball in an international tournament. Naturally, he split the fairway. And won the event. Later, Earl asked him what he was thinking about when he was preparing for that first shot, and Tiger replied that he was thinking where he wanted the ball to go. He was not nervous, nor was he trying not to fail, and perhaps most importantly, he was not worried about what his dad was thinking. Just the shot. There are touring pros out there who will never be able to clear their minds that well.

Earl claims that this is when he really began to understand how good his son could be.

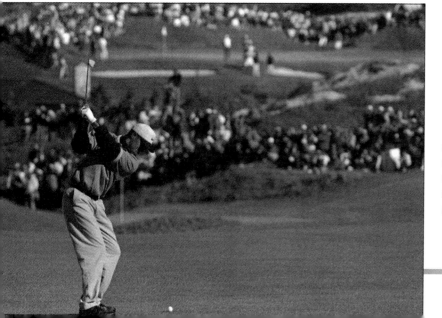

Thanks to Earl's imaginative training methods, Tiger is able to maintain his focus no matter how large or noisy his galleries are.

When Tiger turned seven, Earl felt it was time to start teaching him about mental toughness. Tiger trusted his father enough to know he wouldn't push him too far, and Earl trusted himself to recognize and stay on the right side of that not-so-fine line between Green Beret training and his own homemade golf lessons. Still, he pulled some crazy stuff. Earl would stand 15 feet from Tiger and pretend to be a tree. Tiger would have to chip his shot directly over Earl without drilling him in the forehead. How many kids could do that? While Tiger was hitting his shots, Earl would roll balls into his line of sight, rip at the velcro on his gloves, drop his golf bag, make quick, loud noises or long, soft annoying ones. He would also cheat, and be very conspicuous about it, marking his ball a foot closer to the hole than it was and kicking his ball out of the rough and onto the fairway. When he felt Tiger was nearing the brink, Earl would pull back. Whenever he felt Tiger could take some more, he would step up this psychological warfare. And he told Tiger that any time it got to be too much, all he had to do was say stop. Earl also promised that, if Tiger could take it, he would never meet a golfer that was tougher than he was, and that the gremlins that insinuate themselves into a golfer's mind would never give him a day's worth of trouble.

While Tiger's dad was sowing the seeds that would one day produce an icy, efficient golfing machine, his mother was instilling in Tiger the precepts of Buddhism, a religion that focuses on how to live and interpret the world rather than how not to live and what is right and wrong. Discipline, respect and a nurturing of curiosity were what appealed to Tiger most, and he embraces these aspects of Buddhism to this day. It was also around this time that Tiger probably began to see himself as part of a much bigger picture. The idea that he had some sort of ultimate destiny outside of golf, as his father has often insisted, may not yet have taken root, but certainly he understood that one person could have a great impact on many through a single act. For instance, when the family watched a report on the Ethiopian famine in 1983, Tiger broke into his piggy bank and cracked out a $20 bill.

Tida had no major objections regarding Earl's stoking of Tiger's competitive fire, but she did want her son to understand that Earl was not the only one who could draw lines. She and Tiger would often watch sports together on television, and when an athlete would lose control in a tennis match or a football game, she was quick to remind him of the swift, embarrassing consequences such actions would bring if Tiger ever pulled that kind of crap on the golf course. She would come down from the stands and spank him, she promised, right there in front of everyone. Tiger had no reason to doubt her.

Tiger won his fifth world title at the age of 14.

Earl and Tida were also very conscious about building a foundation of trust and respect with their son. They were careful to promise nothing they could not deliver, and encouraged Tiger to discuss and question anything he did not understand. They also taught him about responsibility. When he started playing golf he would slam his club down when he made a bad shot. Earl would ask him who was to blame for the shot. This helped the boy see that out there on the links, there's no one to blame but yourself.

Thanks to the tag-team mental training of Tida and Earl, Tiger was as focused and cool on a golf course as most players three times his age. At age eight, he won his first club championship, along with the world 10-and-under title at the par-three Presidio Hills Golf Course in San Diego. It was his first of five world titles between 1984 and 1990—two more than anyone else ever won. At age nine, Tiger became totally fixated on lowering his scores. Earl, concerned that he was obsessing on numbers, told him to just relax and have fun. Tiger replied that posting low scores *was* how he had fun, and Earl never bugged him about it again. Finally, by the age of 10, the first phase of Tiger's training was complete. He could already make great shots; but now he had learned how to deal with bad ones. He learned to accept the fact that he had made a mistake, try to understand and correct it, and then move on. Most of the players on the PGA Tour are still grappling with this—Tiger had it pretty well licked by the time his age reached double digits. Today, he "plays angry" about as well as anyone who has ever picked up a club.

> *"I'm going to have some stumbling blocks in my life, but I think with the foundation that my parents have laid down for me I should be able to make it through."*
> **Tiger**

As soon as Tiger reached the big 1-0, he and Earl were back on the Navy Golf Course. The members seemed no more enlightened than they were when Tiger beat their pro at age four, and they tried quietly to find another way to bar him from playing. Meanwhile, Earl was starting to experience health problems. Perhaps the pressure finally took its toll, or maybe it was just a ton too many cheeseburgers, but he suffered a heart attack in 1986. The experience only underscored what Earl and Tida had been telling Tiger all along: work hard and prepare for the future, but don't forget to enjoy today. If you are looking for a reason why Tiger never burned out on golf—or, for that matter, why he did not strangle his parents—look here. Their message was always right on the money.

From that point on, Tiger was, quite literally, unbeatable. During 1987, he entered 30 tournaments in Southern California and won them all. He also began working with golf pro John Anselmo at the Meadowlark Golf Club in Huntington Beach. Anselmo knew he had a prodigy on his hands, but what he appreciated most was that Tiger's parents did not push him relentlessly the way some of his other pupils were pushed. They supported, prodded and challenged Tiger to improve, but let Anselmo do his thing with virtually no interference. Soon, Tiger set his mind on becoming the greatest golfer who ever lived. To the motivational messages posted around his room he added a list of every major championship Jack Nicklaus won. In 1988, when Tiger was 12, Earl retired from his job at McDonnell-Douglas to spend more time on Tiger's career; Tida returned to work full-time as an accountant. A year later, Tiger received his first college recruiting letter, from Stanford University.

In 1989, Earl asked Jay Brunza to join Team Tiger as a sports psychologist. Brunza, a retired captain in the Navy Medical Service Corps, focused on helping Tiger relax and manage his anger as the stakes got higher and higher. He also served as Tiger's caddy in many tournaments. Brunza, too, marveled at the unique parent-child relationship. Tiger was pursuing his own passion, not Earl's or Tida's, and to this day he is convinced that had Tiger decided to quit golf they would have supported him with the same degree of love and commitment.

Tiger spent his early teens playing in weekend tournaments and occasionally traveled out of state—and even out of the country—for bigger events. All the while, Earl pounded home the idea that Tiger was special, that he was put on this earth to do special things. Everything, his father claimed, was practically preordained. Eventually, this became gospel to Tiger. And predictably, he used this potentially counter-productive mantra in the most productive way possible. Instilled with a sense of purpose and destiny, Tiger began to see himself as traveling from point to point on a timeline, with success and prosperity already waiting for him at the end. This made his rare failures easier to deal with—he saw them not as obstacles but as signposts pointing him in the right direction. All he needed to do was understand what went wrong and correct it, and he would be stronger for it. Try explaining that to your typical teenager and see where you get.

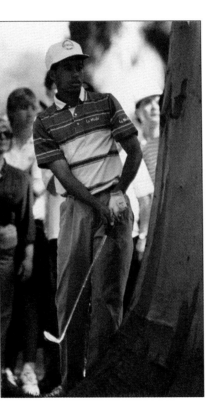

At 16, Tiger became the youngest player ever at a PGA Tour event when he was invited to enter the 1992 L.A. Open.

In 1991, Tiger made the leap from golfing curiosity to national sensation when he won the USGA Junior Championship. At just 15, he was the youngest champion in tournament history, and he nailed down the title in thrilling style, winning on the first hole of sudden death at the Bay Hill Club and Lodge in Orlando, Florida. Later that summer, Tiger barely missed qualifying for the Los Angeles Open. He would have been the youngest golfer ever to play a PGA Tour event. By more than a year.

Although Tiger was not allowed to earn money as an amateur, he learned quickly that he could be a cash cow for his family. Earl was hired by Mark McCormack's International Management Group as a junior golf consultant. Ostensibly, IMG was hiring him to keep them apprised of up-and-coming young golfers. In reality, of course, IMG was angling to curry favor with the family when the time came for Tiger to turn pro. If all went as planned, Tiger could generate upwards of $1 million a year in endorsements from the moment he renounced his amateur status. And if he were to dominate the PGA Tour the way he did the juniors, well, the sky would be the limit. Competing agencies bristled at this blatant skirting of USGA rules, but that's what makes IMG IMG. For his part, Earl said his deal would have no bearing on Tiger's decision when it came time to choose a management company, and promised he would quit as soon as Tiger went to college and he left the junior circuit.

Tiger won the USGA Junior Championship again in 1992, again on the last hole, to become the first two-time winner of the event. Much of the credit for Tiger's success went to swing doctor Butch Harmon, who was hired by Earl when Tiger was 16. Harmon, whose father won the 1948 Masters, never had the temperament to make it on the PGA Tour, but he had the goods when it came to tinkering with pro swings. Greg Norman hired him after he dropped from the Top 50 on the PGA money winners list, and in no time at all, the Shark was number one. Harmon worked with Tiger in person, via phone and fax, and even exchanged videos. He shortened his backswing and tightened Tiger up in some other areas, and put him on a two-hour regimen of weight lifting, aerobics and stretching to add strength and flexibility to what was then a sinewy, 140-pound frame.

> *"He trusted me, and he knew I would never do anything to hurt him."*
> **Earl, on his mental toughness training**

When the Los Angeles Open rolled around again, Tiger did not have to qualify. Thanks to his valiant bid the year before—and his second straight junior title—officials at the Rivera Country Club invited him to play. Thus at the age of 16 years and two months, Tiger became the youngest person ever to play in a PGA Tour event. He also got a little dose of reality, receiving death threats deemed serious enough to assign a special security team to follow him during the tournament. All Tiger did, under this ridiculous pressure, was step up and smack a perfect 280-yard drive off the first tee for his first official shot in a PGA Tour event. A perfect approach and two putts on the par 5 gave him a birdie, and for the first time his name was atop a PGA Tour

"Swing Doctor" Butch Harmon was a key addition to Team Tiger.

leader board. He also got to meet Sam Snead and enjoyed a gallery that swelled to more than 3,000—by far the largest following he had ever experienced.

Alas, Tiger's game was not quite up to pro standards, though his mettle certainly was. On the tournament's second day, his normally accurate drives betrayed him and he shot a 75 to miss the cut. Still, he amplified the other parts of his game, making pars

This resiliency and imagination did not go unnoticed by the experts, who marveled at how Tiger—a 10th grader!—kept his cool even when his bread fell butter-side down. Indeed, the tour pros with whom he partnered observed that his mental game was already PGA-ready, and that his skills, though still unpolished, were already approaching All-America levels.

Tiger began to show signs of his marketing savvy, too, signing autographs with a simple Tiger, and unveiling the mercifully short-lived Tiger Paw gesture when he dropped big putts. When asked if he was disappointed with his showing, Tiger responded that he had had the most fun in his life. When queried on his goals, he said he would like to win a U.S. Amateur title and an NCAA championship. Oh, yes, and the upcoming meet against Gahr High.

For Tiger, 1993 turned out to be a year of growing pains, both literally and figuratively. He stood 6-1—some five inches taller than when he entered

with some creative and daring shots from parts of the course where hackers normally check for witnesses before kicking their balls into better position.

high school—and his body didn't always cooperate with his golf. A chronically sore back and various and sundry muscle pulls sometimes hampered Tiger's game, while at the same time he was going through club lengths like most teenagers go through pepperoni pizzas. On the eve of his last USGA Junior championship, he was still fighting to recover from a bout with mononucleosis. And although Tiger was the overwhelming favorite in the event, he and Earl knew that winning it a third consecutive time would not be easy.

They were correct. Tiger fought his way to the final, where he faced 16-year-old Ryan Armour. He started slowly—normally, no cause for concern, for Tiger was already amateur golf's comeback king—but Armour was playing insane golf, hitting his greens and nailing his putts. With two holes left, Tiger was two down and under the most intense pressure of young career. He drew within one with a birdie, then stepped up to the final hole—a tricky par five—and squeezed off a 300-yard drive. Armour pulled out a long iron, and in doing so issued a challenge to Tiger. He was playing it

safe, going for par; if Tiger wanted to catch him, he would have no choice but to shoot for a birdie.

The strategy seemed sound, especially after Tiger found a fairway bunker with his second shot and Armour played his ball just short of the green. But Tiger sucked it up and chipped his bunker shot about a dozen feet from the hole. He rolled in the birdie to force sudden death, and death came suddenly for the disheartened Armour, who bogeyed the first hole. Tiger got his par and won his third national junior title in a row. In the crowd were coaches from the three schools he was considering: Stanford, Arizona State and UNLV. Visions of sugar plums must have been dancing in their heads.

Tiger's final milestone as a junior came at a qualifying tournament for the U.S. Open. He did not qualify (as it turned out, he did not particularly want to), but he did fire his caddie, and daddy, Earl. Earl was angry with Tiger for tooling him around, and let him know it in no uncertain terms. And then they put it behind them, so both could move on.

Amateur Hour
The Legend Grows

Tiger finished up his senior year at Western High, accepted a scholarship from Stanford University, and embarked upon a journey that would take him to the heights of golf's amateur ranks. His first big win came during the summer of 1994 at the Western Amateur in Michigan, though it nearly cost him a shot at the big prize, the U.S. Amateur. After the Western, Tiger and Earl got caught in traffic on the way to Chicago's O'Hare Airport and missed their flight. There was just one more plane to Florida that day, and it was sold out, so the two waited as standbys, knowing full well that if Tiger could not get a seat, he would not make his tee time. Luckily, the same traffic that worked against Tiger worked for him, and there were enough no-shows so that he and Earl got on.

All eyes were on Tiger during the tournament. He had played it three times before, but now he was expected to win it. Competing against the top adult amateurs and college players in the country, he found the competition much stiffer than in the juniors, but he hung tough after falling three holes down with five to play in the round of sixteen against University of Florida golf coach Buddy Alexander and beat him. Tiger cruised to the finals, where he squared off against University of Oklahoma star Trip Kuehne. There he found himself behind by five holes with 12 to play. Everyone following the pair knew what Tiger had done in the past. During crunch time in countless junior tourneys, he had

> *"In terms of overall impact on the sport...when you figure in media, the dollars on the table for him, his ability to be a role model...if he succeeds, he might be the most important player ever."*
> **PGA Tour Commissioner Tim Finchem**

Tiger's magnificent putt on the 17th hole at Sawgrass gave him his first of three U.S. Amateur titles.

roared past opponents from seemingly impossible deficits, leaving them in slack-jawed awe. But this was different. He was not playing some kid. This was as high as you got in the amateur ranks.

Laying a foundation for future logic-defying performances, Tiger locked into the zone and started knocking down threes like Reggie Miller. He caught Kuehne with just two holes to go, then plopped his tee shot down on Sawgrass's famous island green—with the wind at his back—a mere arm's length away from the water. His mother, who was watching him on TV at home, fell off the bed. Tiger had shot for the right of the pin, where the odds of staying dry are so lousy that most pros wouldn't dream of aiming there. He holed the ensuing 14-footer to take the lead for good, punctuating his comeback with the now-trademark uppercut. And just like that, Tiger was

Tiger dominated college golf while at Stanford, winning the NCAA individual championship as a freshman.

larger than those of all the French golfers combined. One newspaper dubbed him the Mozart of golf. For his part, Tiger credited his fine performance to avoiding rich French foods, admitting that he ate all of his meals at a the McDonalds down the street from the team's hotel.

Back in the states, Tiger put together an impressive freshman resumé. He won his first college event, the Tucker Invitational in New Mexico, and midway through his first year he became the number-one ranked collegiate golfer in the world. He also did for college golf what he had done for the junior and amateur circuits, attracting thousands of fans to events that had once been played before just a few hundred spectators. While competing in the Thunderbird Collegiate Invitational in Tempe, Tiger caused such a stir that gallery ropes had to be used for the first time in tournament history. The scene was similar at every event in which the Stanford squad was entered. Tiger even stole the attention from other top

the youngest champion of the oldest golf tournament in the United States.

A couple of weeks after enrolling at Stanford, Tiger was on the road again, in France, helping the U.S. win its first World Amateur Team Championship in more than a decade. He played well under pressure and logged some valuable international experience. And of course, he was the most watched, most photographed and most followed player at the tournament. In fact, Tiger's gallery was college golfers, including the entire Oklahoma State squad, which top-to-bottom ranks as one of the finest in history. The tradeoff, however, was acceptable, for although Tiger overshadowed everyone else, his presence threw the national spotlight on a heretofore underappreciated and practically unknown part of the sport.

In the spring of 1995, Tiger played his first Masters, gaining an exemption thanks to his U.S. Amateur title the summer before. He became only the fourth person of color to qualify for the event, which did not see its first black entrant until Lee Elder played the tournament in 1975. Tiger had been invited to play the course before, but had always politely turned down the offers. He did not want to go to Augusta until he earned the right to play there. Once he knew he was going, however, it was all he could think about. During Christmas break in 1994, he studied videos of past Masters broadcasts and tried to pick up some of the nuances of the course, which is perfect for long drivers but murder on those who lack finesse with short irons and on the greens. He brought the tapes back to Stanford in January of 1995 and watched them regularly until the tournament in April.

Ray Floyd (left) and Greg Norman got a glimpse of the future when they watched Tiger blast 300-yard drives prior to the 1995 Masters.

The media was all over the place when Tiger arrived. An 18-year-old black golfer playing the Masters was quite a story, and during the days leading up to the first round he was asked over and over how he felt and what he thought. Well aware of the club's exclusionary practices, Tiger was careful not to be too effusive in his praise, but inside he was like a kid in a candy store. What made the whole experience even more fun was that the top names in golf were falling all over themselves for the chance to play with Tiger. During the three days prior to round one, he played with Nick Faldo, Raymond Floyd, Nick Price and Gary Player. In practice rounds, Tiger regularly outdrove longball artists Greg Norman and Fred Couples by a good 30 yards. He also received a good luck telegram from black golf pioneer Charlie Sifford, whom he regarded as something of a grandfather figure. Sifford advised Tiger to concentrate on playing the course, and to ignore the media circus surrounding his appearance.

Earl recreated his old role of caddie-daddy, and for the first two days of the tournament, Tiger and his father were all anyone wanted to talk about. During the tournament, Tiger averaged 311 yards per drive—14 more than John Daly. Despite overshooting many of the greens, he scored a pair of 72s the first two days and raised plenty of eyebrows with his play and his demeanor. Following his second round, he visited the nearby Forest Hills Golf Club and managed to sneak in a clinic for a group of black children before the sun went down. He also spoke with a group of Augusta's black caddies, who had been bumped from their usual jobs during the Masters by the personal caddies hired by many of the pros.

Tiger was hopping mad with his short game during his first visit to Augusta.

Playing in the 1995 British Open was a turning point for Tiger.

They asked Tiger if he thought a black golfer might ever win the Masters. He personally guaranteed that one would.

Back at the club, Tiger was neither awestruck nor disrespectful, and in fact seemed strangely at home in a place that had slammed the door on so many black golfers during the previous six decades (and a town whose inhabitants saw fit to smash a window on Earl and Tida's rental car without bothering to steal anything). As has long been the tradition, the U.S. Amateur champion was housed on the second floor of the club itself; not until it was all over did Tiger admit that he had been sneaking down into the clubhouse at night, nosing around, reveling in the history and soaking up the atmosphere.

After his freshman year at Stanford, Tiger traveled to Great Britain, where he played the Scottish Open and British Open. There he began to understand that, to fulfill his potential, he would need to expand his arsenal beyond the breathtaking drives that turned par-fives into par-threes. Winning against the likes of Greg Norman and Nick Faldo would mean controlling the ball on the ground and in the air, not just knocking the bejesus out of it. Playing the treacherous, windswept courses at

Earl was the first to congratulate Tiger after he downed George Marucci for his second straight U.S. Amateur Championship.

Carnoustie and St. Andrews, Tiger got a taste of what he could expect as a touring pro, and a preview of the kind of golf he would have to play to defend his U.S. Amateur title come summer. The tournament was returning to its birthplace, the tricky seaside links at Newport, Rhode Island, and Tiger aimed to become only the ninth golfer in history to win back-to-back amateur championships.

As it turned out, this one was a little easier than his big '94 win, though no less tense, as he had to overcome a pair of wily 43-year-old veterans, each of whom took Tiger to the very last hole before succumbing. Against eight-time Maine state champion Mark Plummer in the semifinal, Tiger had to be super solid to escape with a victory. Against Buddy Marucci, he needed to be better than that. After 19 holes, the four-time Pennsylvania state champ had Tiger down two. But Tiger roared back to go up one. On the final hole, Marucci, landed a pretty shot to within birdie range—if Tiger bogeyed, there would be a playoff. Tiger responded with a ball he could not have hit a few months before: a delicate half-shot that floated over the pin and then spun back to within a foot and a half of the cup. Marucci, a beaten man, offered his hand to Tiger as the two walked to the green. If he had to lose to a kid, it was an honor to be beaten with a big-time shot like that. After the tournament, Earl Woods made a toast to his son, and predicted that he would win 14 major championships as a pro. Though no one in their wildest dreams could imagine it, he was less than two years away from his first.

Upon his return to Stanford in the fall of '95, Tiger started logging time in the weight room. A long hitter to begin with, he tacked on major yardage to his shots as he added dense muscle to his lanky frame. Tiger got bigger, and more importantly, stronger—and there is no substitute for strength in golf. The athletic department's weight room supervisor claimed that, pound-for-pound, Tiger was one of the strongest athletes on campus. Within a couple of seasons, he would rank among the strongest golfers in the world. By the end of Tiger's sophomore year, he could hit balls completely over most doglegs, making a mockery out of some of the best-designed courses in the country.

In the summer of 1996, Tiger returned to the British Open. After stumbling through the first round, he shot a marvelous second-round 66. It was at this point that he first considered leaving school and turning pro. Something had changed that day. The game suddenly seemed clearer than ever to him, and his mind and body clicked into perfect harmony. Also,

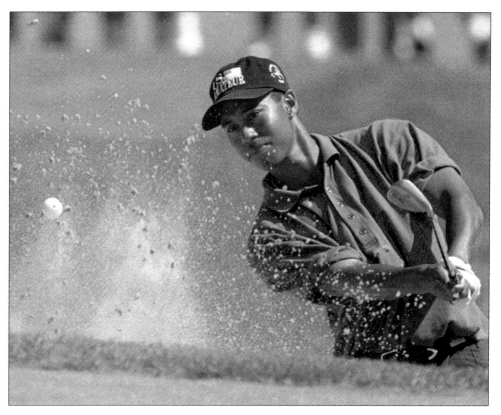

A sparkling bunker shot enabled Tiger to beat Stanford teammate Joel Kribel in a close semifinal at the 1996 U.S. Amateur.

he had accomplished everything he could at the junior and college levels, and it was getting harder and harder to motivate himself for tournaments that seemed below his ever-improving level of play. Tiger vowed to join the PGA Tour if he captured his third straight U.S. Amateur title in August.

Naturally, the experts inserted Tiger as the favorite at the '96 Amateur. Based on his dramatic comeback victories the two previous years, the prevailing wisdom dictated that he would register a relatively easy win at Pumpkin Ridge, Oregon. But Joel Kribel and Steve Scott had something to say about that. Kribel, his Stanford teammate, was Tiger's opponent in the semifinal round of match play, and he sprinted to a two-up lead after just four holes. Tiger pulled even and then won it on the final nine, with an eagle and two birdies, including a magnificent bunker shot on 10.

Against the 19-year-old Scott, Tiger dropped four holes on the front nine of the 36-hole final. With 15,000 fans roaring after each shot (good or bad) Tiger struggled to find his game. Meanwhile, Scott played solidly. After 20 holes, the difference was five—the same deficit Tiger overcame in 1994 against Trip Kuehne. As the afternoon wore on, Tiger started booming his drives and rolling in his long putts. On the 28th hole, a 535-yard par five, he hit a 350-yard drive, lifted a five-iron to within 45 feet of the cup, and then curled in a lovely putt for an eagle.

To his credit, Scott refused to fold, but Tiger was too good, catching him on the 35th hole with another impossibly long putt after a less-than-perfect approach. They halved 36 to force sudden death, and Scott nearly won the championship on the first extra hole, missing an 18-footer by inches. On the next hole, a par-three, Tiger put his tee shot within 12 feet of the pin, while Scott buried his in the rough. Tiger putted out for par to win. It was the most dramatic final anyone involved with the tournament could remember.

Tiger and his parents agreed he should go pro while the getting was good, and Earl let the world know that the bidding could commence. There would be a very limited number of endorsements for Tiger, at least at first, and he was expecting somewhere between top dollar and Michael Jordan money to put his name and game behind someone's product. And he got it: a combined $60 million from Nike—which was longing to grab a bigger piece of golf's footwear and apparel markets—and Titleist, which added Tiger to its impressive stable of golfing thoroughbreds. Fans were agog at the numbers, but what impressed the pros was Tiger's ability to shut out all of the noise and commotion of a huge gallery and just focus on making the shot. That was the big tipoff that he was ready to make his presence felt on the PGA Tour.

> **"It was time for me to go, and I was ready to go."**
> **Tiger on turning pro at age 20**

Sudden Impact
Tiger Hits the Tour

Tiger's first stroke as a pro came with a pen, not a club, in his hand. He made out a check for the $3,000 entry fee to the PGA Tour Qualifying Tournament, a December event that represents the last chance for golfers to crack the show for the following year. It seems a bit silly in retrospect, but with just a handful of events left in the 1996 season, there was a very real chance that Tiger would not be able to golf his way into the Top 125, and that was where he needed to be to get his PGA Tour card for 1997. As an amateur, he had never finished better than 22nd in a PGA event, leading some to believe he would struggle during his first year or two on the tour. For his part, Tiger was simply playing it safe when he handed over the check. When he played those pro tournaments he was in school, sometimes writing papers and studying for exams between rounds. Without those distractions, he expected to get into a groove right away. In fact, he had

his sights on at least one win in '96, and wanted desperately to make the 1997 Ryder Cup team.

Tiger's first tournament was the Greater Milwaukee Open, one of the many late-season PGA events that generally attract sparse crowds, few big names and dismal TV ratings. The presence of golf's most celebrated rookie, however, changed all that. Tiger drew a huge and enthusiastic gallery, as well as a record number of writers, reporters and television crews. His first shot as a pro was a breathtaking drive that rolled to a stop more than 335 yards from the tee. Tiger missed some makeable putts during the round, but made enough spectacular shots to finish with a very respectable 67. He was five strokes off the lead, behind first-round leader Nolan Henke, who carded a tournament-record 62 in more or less complete privacy.

During the tournament, the gallery was so focused on Tiger that few realized that, standing among them, was Hall-of-Fame baseball player Hank Aaron. In his first season in Milwaukee, he too had given local fans reason to ooh and aah, producing rocket shots with an eerily similar, whippet-like 20-year-old frame. Every time Tiger launched a tee shot, Aaron could not help but laugh. He knows what it is to have that magic. And he knows what it is to play under intense scrutiny. Through his dark glasses and past the bill of his pulled-down golf cap, he surely saw a little bit of himself out there.

Tiger stayed close for another round, but all those 36-hole days at the U.S. Amateur began to catch up with him and he dropped out of contention in the third round. He finished the tournament tied for 60th, but knocked down a hole-in-one on the last day to reward the thousands of fans who had followed him all four days. When Tiger received his prize money check for $2,544, it was one of the proudest moments in his life. Unlike the mind-numbing millions he was due to receive in endorsement contracts, this was money that he had actually gone out and earned himself. Having never worked a day in his

Tiger had to see the ball for himself after his hole-in-one at the Greater Milwaukee Open.

life—not by choice or privilege, but by Earl and Tida's design—it was a unique feeling. For his troubles, Tiger was also the proud owner of a ranking of 346. And so began the Tiger Watch.

From a golf standpoint, the GMO was not a total loss. Indeed, Tiger's crummy third round, in some ways, was his most impressive. His game was off and he shot a 73, but it could have been far worse. Most newcomers—and, for that matter, many veterans—tend to back off when their game suddenly becomes unreliable. But Tiger never wavered, never lost his cool. His response was not to salvage the day, but to do whatever he had to in order to stay in the hunt. To the great delight of his gallery (which easily outnumbered all of the other galleries combined) he attempted, and made, some gutsy recovery shots. Those who predicted that he might not immediately find his way on the tour had to admit that he handled himself beautifully. As for Tiger's impact on the PGA Tour, there was little question that things were about to change. In a scene right out of a Beatles movie, Tiger's fans camped outside his hotel and screamed until he came to the window to acknowledge their cheers. Defending champ Scott Hoch went virtually ignored. The only person camped outside his room was probably a member of the housekeeping staff.

With the hubbub of his first tournament out of the way, Tiger jetted over to Toronto to play the Canadian Open. He shot three good rounds and finished eight under, earning an 11th place tie, a check for $37,500, and a bump up to 204 in the rankings. Five days later he was atop the leader board at the Quad City Classic in Illinois, and in position to take the tournament after 36 holes. Tiger held off his challengers in round three, but hit a speed bump on his way to the championship with a quadruple bogey on the final day that sent him tumbling into a tie for fifth. The media, all geared up to anoint Tiger as the second coming of Jack Nicklaus, had to pull back at the last minute, and some reporters assumed a told-ya-so stance. This, they pointed out, was one of those inevitable lessons Tiger would be learning about the pitfalls of the PGA Tour. One bad hole and you're history. This pearl of wisdom was directed at the hundreds of thousands of new fans that Tiger had attracted to the game, not Tiger himself. If anyone understood how disastrous a quadruple bogey could be, it was he. What the experts failed to

Tiger finished a respectable fifth at the Quad City Classic, but he knew he had let his first PGA victory slip from his grasp.

add was that dealing with this kind of disappointment is in many ways the mark of an emerging champion. And Tiger proved he had the ability to bounce back by finishing third in his very next tournament, the British Columbia Open. He shot a near-flawless 68, 66 and 66 to end up 13-under and climb to 128 in the rankings. Would, as many were now predicting, Tiger win his next event?

As it turned out, he would not even play it. Physically exhausted and mentally drained, Tiger backed out of the Buick Challenge in Georgia, turning down a prized sponsor's exemption a day before the tournament was to start. Though disappointed, tournament officials tried hard to understand. But when Tiger also announced that he planned to skip the Haskins Award dinner—a dinner held to honor Tiger as the nation's top collegiate golfer for 1996—he incurred the wrath of the entire golf community. Some of the game's greats went on record saying that Tiger had made a monumental

Tiger got a standing ovation for his heartfelt apology when he accepted the 1996 Haskins Award as the nation's top collegiate golfer.

blunder. You can earn a nice living and generate a lot of good will in golf if you remember who butters your bread. Cancelling out on a $150-a-plate dinner when you are the guest of honor is remarkably bad form.

If there was a lesson to be learned about life on the pro tour, it was from the subsequent outpouring of negativity that followed. In the wake of Affaire d'Haskins, columnists across the country lashed out against Tiger, claiming the rookie had violated some sort of a sacred code. And even the most objective newspapers and magazines seemed to take a certain satisfaction in the fact that Tiger had finally done something stupid. A lot of people who had looked Tiger in the eye, shook his hand and warmly wished him luck were suddenly spewing venom in the press about how immature, unprepared and insensitive he was. Tiger quickly admitted his mistake, wrote personal apologies to the 200 attendees, and rescheduled the dinner.

The PGA Tour and its fans do not forgive, nor do they forget. Unless, of course, you win. Proving the adage that living well is the best revenge, Tiger went out to Nevada the very next week and tore up the course at the Las Vegas Invitational. He began with a 70, then shot a mind-boggling 26 under over the next three rounds. To put this performance into its proper perspective, consider that the PGA record for four rounds is just one stroke better, 27 under. And he did it in eye-popping style. Tiger's driving average for the tournament was 323 yards—more than 38 yards better than the field's average—despite a groin injury that made him grimace after nearly every shot.

Less than two weeks earlier, Tiger and Davis Love III had played a practice round together prior to the Buick Challenge, and Tiger said it would be pretty cool if, at some time in the future, the two of them went down to the wire in a tournament.

> *"He is obviously the next great player...I think everybody better watch out. He's going to be a force. He knows what he's doing. He's great for the PGA Tour."*
> **Davis Love III**

Tiger earned $297,000 and a two-year exemption with his first victory as a pro.

In Vegas, Love must have felt as if he were playing against the gods as he watched Tiger scratch and claw his way toward him on the final day from an impossible seven strokes down. Tiger caught Love on the very last hole and forced a sudden-death playoff, then beat him on the very next hole for his first tour victory. Tiger now stood 40th on the money-winners list, he was $297,000 richer, and he had himself a two-year exemption.

The Texas Open was up next, but the excitement and commotion surrounding Tiger's great win was more distracting than he anticipated. Companies that had shied away at first were now ready to pony up big bucks for Tiger, and offers of astronomical appearance fees were rolling in from all over the world. Media requests went through the roof, and scheduling dilemmas were beginning to crop up all over the place. No one had anticipated Tiger would get so big so fast, and Team Tiger was caught off guard. The original plan had been for the young star to discuss everything

Though distracted during the Texas Open, Tiger's fine work around the greens enabled him to secure his fourth straight Top 5 finish.

with his dad, his attorney and his agent between tournaments. But in the days following Las Vegas, there just was not time to cover everything. When Tiger took to the course in Texas, there was still a huge amount of unfinished business on his mind, and clearly it was affecting his game. It got so bad at one point that he screamed at Earl as if he were a low-level employee. Somehow, Tiger managed to finish third, banking another very hefty paycheck and rising six more notches on the money list. But the most positive thing to come out of the tournament was a new protocol for his company. From that point on, Earl would set up a weekly teleconference with Tiger's advisors, sort through everything, and then present Tiger with only the most crucial decisions. With that out of the way, Tiger got back to concentrating on golf, and the family flew to Orlando for the Walt Disney World/Oldsmobile Classic.

Tiger shared the spotlight with—who else?—Tigger after his win at the Disney Classic.

The Disney was Tiger's seventh tournament, and he was riding a streak of four straight Top 5 finishes. To say that anticipation was high would be a gross understatement. Attendance for the event was better than triple what it had been in 1995, and when the tournament director first heard that Tiger was definitely coming he was so overjoyed that he jumped fully clothed into his swimming pool. This event, more than the first six, offered an intriguing glimpse into the nature of Tiger's celebrity. As one might expect, there were more black and brown faces in the gallery than ever before. But the galleries were also swelled by blue-collar moms and dads, and thousands of kids who wouldn't have been caught dead on a golf course only a couple of months before. Despite a nagging case of the sniffles, Tiger played wonderfully. He shot 69, 63 and 69 to start the fourth day just one shot off the lead, then roared through the

Tiger found himself playing a lot of shots from the rough after Earl's heart attack during the Tour Championships in Tulsa.

final 18 holes with a 66 that was good enough for his second victory in three tournaments.

After seven professional events, the golf world began to look closely at what it had in Tiger Woods. He had joined the tour's Top 25 in record time. Also, he had recorded five straight Top 5 finishes. No one had pulled that off since 1982, and no first-year player had ever done it. Tiger had shot in the 60s in 21 of his first 27 rounds as a pro, and birdied more than half of the par fives he had encountered. He had also invigorated the tail end of the PGA Tour, increasing total attendance by at least 150,000 for tournaments that desperately needed the exposure and cash. And he had won a couple of tournaments. No, they were not majors. But Tiger was not beating pushovers, either. Besides besting Love, he humbled several PGA superstars, including Ernie Els, Fred Couples, Corey Pavin, Phil Mickelson and Mark O'Meara. And he was doing it in a decisive manner, playing aggressive shots from bad lies, holing key putts when he had to, and out-driving all of the game's heavy hitters.

At the Tour Championships in Tulsa the following week, an alarming dose of reality brought Tiger's fantasy season to a grinding halt. Between the first and second rounds, Earl suffered another heart attack and was rushed to a local hospital. Tiger was at his side through most of the night, until he was assured that his father was stable and out of danger. Perhaps remembering the fallout from his no-show at the Buick Challenge, Tiger returned to the course on a couple of hours sleep and slogged his way to a

78, but recovered on the last two days to shoot par and finish in a tie for 21st.

Tiger took three weeks off to be with his dad and catch his own breath, then returned to play in the Australian Open, where he finished tied for fifth. He also played the Skins Game with John Daly, Tom Watson and Fred Couples, then teamed with Kelli Kuehne—sister of Trip Kuehne, his nemesis at the 1994 U.S. Amateur—to place second at the JCPenney Classic and pocket $75,000 to close out the most remarkable rookie season in the history of the sport.

Tiger was a crowd pleaser at the JCPenney Classic, where he teamed with Kelli Kuehne.

Tiger finished nine rounds short of the minimum 50 to qualify for official leadership in the various PGA categories, but in no way did this minor point take away from his numbers. He averaged 302.8 yards per drive, the highest mark in golf history over a span of 10 tournaments. He recorded 13 eagles—just three off the tour lead—and played a total of 26.8% of his holes under par, which was four points better than the official tour leader, Joe Ozaki. As good as Tiger's stats were, however, they could have been even better. By his own admission, he had not putted well during any of the tournaments he played, including the two he won.

As 1996 drew to a close, the great debate in golf was whether Tiger Woods had been on a hot streak, or whether he was really that good, and getting better. For many golf aficionados, the latter was too much to comprehend. If he was already as good as his 1996 performance suggested,

> ### *"He's been thrown into the deep end, believe me. Major champions haven't had to do that, you know."*
> **Ernie Els on the media circus Tiger faced turning pro**

then he belonged in the pantheon of golfing legends—Nicklaus, Palmer, Hogan, Jones—some 10 years before a great golfer typically reaches his prime. Naturally, stories began popping up everywhere about potential problems in his game, the injury risk associated with hitting the ball so hard, and how the law of averages was bound to catch up with him in '97 (the sophomore jinx, as it were). Also, some believed the pressure factor would begin to wear on Tiger—the pressure of being a global celebrity, the pressure of having everyone else gunning for you, the pressure of simply maintaining such a high level of play. The country's sports talk stations, though hardly a touchstone for intelligent golf discussion, joined the chorus of nay-sayers when Tiger was selected as *Sports Illustrated* Athlete of the Year. What had he done? Won a couple of tournaments? To a lot of team sports people, Tiger's quick start was strictly flash-in-the-pan material.

The throngs at the first tee of the Mercedes Championships were typical of Tiger's following during 1997.

This is where a lot of people missed the point. Or ignored it. Earl Woods had started preparing his kid for this moment when he was seven. Tiger's Green Beret training was designed to keep his mind calm and clear no matter how much pressure there was. All he had to do in 1997 was go out and play golf. Mental toughness, focus—these were unlikely to be at issue. If he played well, he would win. For his part, Tiger began the year by thinking big. He was thinking about taking the Masters.

The first stop was January's Mercedes Championships, the reincarnation of the old Tournament of Champions, where the previous year's event-winners slugged it out against one another to kick off the new season. Tiger stayed in the hunt for the first couple of rounds with scores of 70 and 67, then kicked it into overdrive at the end of the third with birdies on each of the final four holes to tie Tom Lehman for the lead. On the 569-yard 17th, Tiger erased any lingering doubt that pressure would derail him in 1997 when he blasted his tee shot a mile, then pulled a three wood out of his bag. It told the crowd he was going for the green in two (something no one had done on this hole), and they gave him a loud ovation. It was a new first for Tiger, and maybe even for golf. Had a gallery ever applauded something so mundane as a club selection? Tiger played the ball perfectly, rolling it to within a few yards of the hole to set up an easy birdie.

The timing of Tiger's late charge proved propitious, as the final day's play was rained out. As the rain continued Monday, tourney officials hit on the idea of a one-hole playoff,

Tiger finished off Tom Lehman with a dead-on six iron in the one-hole playoff that decided the Mercedes winner.

and selected the par-three seventh hole—a little ploy which negated Tiger's power advantage. So what happened? Lehman, hitting first, plopped his ball in the water on the left side. Tiger, knowing the event was all but his, nevertheless made a couple of last-second adjustments and almost knocked the ball in with a soft six iron. He pocketed $296,000 and a new Benz, which he gave to Tida, and started the year he was supposed "come down to earth" as the top-ranked golfer on the planet.

Tiger played two additional tournaments in January. He finished a disappointing 18th at the Phoenix Open, but added some footage to his highlight reel with a hole-in-one that brought the house down. He then rebounded at the AT&T Pebble Beach National Pro-Am, nearly winning it, despite opening the event with two mediocre rounds. Tiger got back into the thick of things with a third-round 63 and a fourth-round 64, and gave

Tiger was paired with Tin Cup star Kevin Costner during the 1997 Pebble Beach Pro-Am.

the fans chills on the tournament's final two holes, as he tried desperately to make up three strokes on Mark O'Meara. At the par three 17th, Tiger landed his tee shot to within inches of the pin; on the monster par-five 18th, he did the undoable by reaching the green in two. O'Meara, who seemed on the verge of a heart attack, watched Tiger's eagle putt just miss, dropping him into a second-place tie.

alf a planet away, in Thailand, officials from the Honda Invitational prepared for Tiger's arrival. The Honda is a stop normally reserved for those trying to cut their teeth on the Asian Tour, but to Tiger the tournament represented a wonderful opportunity to acknowledge his heritage and honor his mother. It also gave Thai fans a chance to see their favorite athlete in person. Tiger has been immensely popular in Thailand long before he turned pro. In fact, his 1996 U.S. Amateur victory was rerun on television six times before the Honda, and the season before, popular NFL broadcasts had been interrupted so that his victories at Las Vegas and Orlando could be shown live.

> *"I've said for a while that somebody was going to come along with the ability to hit it as long as we do and get it in the fairway, and that guy is going to rewrite the books. Guess what? He's here."*
>
> **Art Sellinger, National Long-Driving Champion**

By PGA Tour standards, the first-place money was chump change (and he had already received a fat guarantee just for showing) but as always Tiger came to play. He even partnered up with local dignitaries and business big wigs in the Wednesday pro-am. Ironically, this almost proved his undoing, as the dramatic shifts in time and temperature contributed to an alarming case of heat exhaustion. Still a bit groggy in the opening round, Tiger stroked his way to a 70, then pulled away with scores of 64, 66 and 68 for an easy 10-stroke victory.

Tida was the proudest mother in Thailand when Tiger won the Honda Classic.

> *"Our selection of Tiger is not based on the assumption that he's going to win countless major championships. In my mind, he doesn't have to win another tournament to be a most deserving Sportsman of the Year. His game, his dramatic victories, his competitive nature and his enormous impact on the sport—both on and off the golf course—make him a compelling selection."*
> **Bill Colson, Sports Illustrated**

After playing the Australian Masters in Melbourne, Tiger returned to the PGA Tour and began focusing on the things he needed to do to win the Masters. He and Harmon worked on controlling his irons and putts, and inserted subtle adjustments in his game. Tiger put these changes into play at his next three tournaments—the Nissan Open, Bay Hill Invitational (the site of his first U.S. Junior title) and the Players Championship at Sawgrass (where he won the 1994 Amateur)—with mixed results. He shot a combined twelve under par, but finished in the Top 10 only at Bay Hill. This led to a lot of conjecture that Tiger was not ready for the Masters. He had been leaving his putts short, especially at TPC, and that kind of miscalculation, said the best minds in golf, would kill him at Augusta. But he and Harmon knew something the best minds did not: Tiger was not slumping. The greens at Sawgrass were much slower than those at Augusta, and Tiger was merely experimenting with a different stroke to control the pace of his putts. Indeed, by the time he reached Augusta, Tiger had actually *sharpened* his game.

Tiger got into a little trouble at the Bay Hill Invitational, causing some to predict that he would get eaten alive at Augusta.

Young Master

Tiger's First Major

Master Blaster or Master Disaster? That was what the galleries at Augusta were wondering as they watched Tiger tumble down the leader board on the first nine holes of the 1997 Masters. Greatness, it seemed would have to wait. Tiger's driving betrayed him, leading to four bogeys on the front nine for a score of 40. Those who had picked Tiger to win went scrambling back to the record book to see if it could still be done. What they found was that the worst front nine ever by a Masters winner was a 38. Tiger would have to make history if he planned to pull this baby out of the fire.

The back nine, however, was a different story. He shortened his backswing to gain more control (just the kind of on-the-fly correction most pros are loathe to make) and then suddenly Tiger was Tiger again. He began to undo the damage immediately, birdying 10 with an 18-foot putt and nailing a two on the par-three 12th hole with a magnificent chip from the fringe. He birdied 13 and eagled the par-five 15th, then racked up one more birdie to complete the back nine with a staggering score of 30. After a disastrous start, Tiger was just three strokes off the lead.

> *"I never thought Tiger was going to have any difficulty on tour...but it's not because of his golf swing, or in spite of it. To become a first-class player, the swing is fourth on the priority list behind the head, the heart and the stomach."*
>
> **Pete Kostis, TV Commentator**

Tiger's second shot at **15** led to an eagle
and keyed a remarkable back-nine
score of **30** on the first day.

*Tiger played with tournament favorite Nick Faldo
in the first round. Incredibly, the Englishman
would miss the cut the next day.*

By the end of the second round, Tiger was in command. He shot the best 18 holes of the day, carding a 66, which was good for a three-stroke lead over Colin Montgomerie. Two potential challengers —Nick Faldo and Greg Norman—were out of the picture, having missed the cut. If Tiger could bear down and just play his game, the tournament was in the bag.

Easier said than done, claimed the experts. This was not Las Vegas or Bangkok. This was Augusta. Some of golf's greatest champions had come unglued and coughed up secure leads under the intense pressure of the Masters.

Tiger's second-round 66 was the best score of the day.

> *"I think Tiger's performance has got everyone feeling that they have to improve or get left behind."*
> **Tom Lehman,**
> **1996 PGA Tour Player of the Year**

Tiger's focus on the greens at Augusta was magnificent. He did not bogey a single hole on the back nine throughout the tournament.

By the end of the third day, Tiger was well on the way to shattering more than a half-dozen scoring records at Augusta.

And so he went out and just plain lit up the course. Tiger played every hole par or better, opening a nine-stroke lead with a numbingly perfect 65. No one doubted Tiger's ability to hold on to the lead during the final round. There was no more proving to be done. He had overwhelmed the course, mangled his opponents, and played as if the swarming, buzzing gallery wasn't even there. All that remained were records to be broken, ghosts to be disturbed.

Tiger's great performance, the fulfilling of his destiny as it were, had a weird effect on the other golfers. The usual grimness that accompanies the eve of the final round was gone, replaced by a sort of bewildered jocularity. Despite all of Tiger's advanced billing, no one could quite believe what they had just seen. And no one could wait to see what the 21-year-old would do to the course the next day. There was no question that he would become the tournament's youngest champion, but would he also be its most dominant?

One can scarcely imagine what went through Tiger's head that Saturday night. Earl told him that the last round might be one of the toughest he would ever play. The expectations would be monumental, the crowds boisterous, and the course as treacherous as always. Greg Norman had held a huge lead just a year earlier going into Sunday's final round, and he was overwhelmed, finishing an embarrassing five shots off the pace. If ever there was a time when Dad's mental toughness drills would come into play, this was it.

The next day, Tiger saw his lead drop by a stroke early on as he birdied two, but bogeyed five and seven. He then birdied eight with a remarkable bump-and-run shot after a less-than-perfect swing off the tee. He finished the front nine at even par, but his birdie on eight seemed to lock him in. Tiger sank birdie putts on three of the next five holes. The record for largest margin of victory was all but his, and the mark for lowest score only required pars on the final four holes. There was a tense moment on 16 when Tiger needed, and dropped, a difficult putt; and an errant drive on 18, which

Tiger's final round pulled the largest television ratings in Masters history.

Tiger's great recovery shot on 18 enabled him to break the scoring record held by Jack Nicklaus and Ray Floyd.

required a delicate pitch to the green to save par, but the tournament was never in doubt.

Waiting for Tiger at 18 was Tom Kite, who had secured the third second-place finish of his career at Augusta. It is not unusual in any tournament for the runner-up to hang around while the leader finishes behind him. You never know what could happen. But Kite, 12 strokes back, knew nothing short of a lightning bolt could vault him into first place. He was waiting there for the same reason as everyone else: to watch history being made.

> *"Arnold and I agreed that you could take his Masters wins and my Masters wins, add them together and he should win more than both of us."*
> **Jack Nicklaus**

After holing out on 18, the new Masters champ threw his trademark upper cut.

By the time Tiger slipped on the green jacket, he was the proud owner of a couple of the sport's most cherished records. His 18-under 270 was the best in tournament history. The last time someone won a major by more strokes, golf had not reached these shores, and the slaves had not yet been emancipated. More amazing perhaps was how Tiger achieved those numbers. He was hitting seven-irons and wedges onto the greens while his pursuers were trying to catch him with five-irons and three-woods. Tiger's driving was breathtaking in its distance and accuracy. He averaged 323 yards per drive; no one else broke 300. He played the back nine 16 strokes under par over the four days to shatter Arnold Palmer's 35-year-old record of 12-under, and shot a cumulative 13-under on Augusta's tricky par-5's. On the back nine, Tiger

Tiger's final-round partner, Constantino Rocca, was one of three future Ryder Cup opponents he played with at Augusta.

> *"I thought I would not attain this much success until probably about twenty-three. But I kind of surpassed my own expectations."*
> **Tiger on his Masters win**

Earl, who was not well enough to follow Tiger
around the course, was waiting for him
with a bear hug as he came off 18.

> *"Tiger Woods is all he was previously labeled and more...I've witnessed a lot of green jacket presentations in my time, but none fit better than Tiger's."*
> **Brent Musberger,**
> **ESPN Radio**

did not shoot a single bogey for the entire tournament. During rounds two and three—when the men are traditionally separated from the boys—Tiger shot a 66 followed by a 65; only one other entrant shot a 66 on either day. During those 36 holes he drove not only with great power, but with startling consistency, hitting 26 of 28 fairways and almost always positioning himself for an easy chip to the cup. Indeed, throughout the tournament, the longest club he used on any par-four all week was a seven-iron! Tiger was, of course, the first minority golfer to win the Masters— and the first, in fact, to win a major tournament. He supplanted Seve Ballesteros as the event's youngest winner, and he was the youngest winner of a major since Gene Sarazen took the 1922 U.S. Open and PGA Championship at the age of 20. Tiger's drawing power also set a couple of Masters records. Officially, the television ratings for the event were the highest in history, and unofficially, scalpers were getting record prices—up to $10,000 for a weekly badge.

In the past, when asked how much better he could be, Tiger always answered that he had yet to play an

> *"Unless they build Tiger tees about fifty yards back, he's going to win the next twenty of these."*
> **Jesper Parnevik**

In a tradition dating back more than six decades,
defending Masters champion Nick Faldo
presented Tiger with his green jacket.

entire tournament with his "A" game. The 1997 Masters, he admitted, was pretty close. Of course, that is what separates the great golfers from the very good ones. Winning a tournament when all of the pieces just won't come together is a special gift shared only by the Nicklauses, Palmers and Hogans of the world. What separates Tiger from them, however, is who he is and where he comes from. His thoughts on the final hole, as he strode down the fairway with fans bowing to him as he passed, are revealing. When asked what was going through his mind, Tiger replied that he whispered a prayer of thanks to Charlie Sifford, Lee Elder, Teddy Rhodes and golf's other black pioneers who opened up the sport so he could play.

Tiger proved a gracious, warm and respectful champion. He also acknowledged who he is and where he came from in an imaginative and touching way. Going into the final round, he chose to wear a red shirt and black pants, knowing he would almost certainly be adding a green jacket to that combination. Red, green and black are the colors of African nationalism. And on his way to the clubhouse after closing the deal, he laid a bear hug on Lee Elder and thanked him for making this day possible. A final, poignant reminder of what Tiger's win represented came as he entered the dining room for the winner's dinner. He was received with the heartfelt applause normally accorded the

tournament champ, but this time it was just a little louder. This time the Augusta kitchen staff, in the back of the room, joined in the ovation, clapping long and hard for a champion who had been in the making far longer than 21 years.

Two days later, on April 15th, the nation honored Jackie Robinson by commemorating the 50th anniversary of the day he played his first game for the Brooklyn Dodgers. President

Lee Elder was in Tiger's thoughts as he marched up the 18th fairway, and in his arms after the tournament

Clinton invited the new Masters champion to attend a special ceremony at Shea Stadium, where the Mets were playing the Dodgers. An exhausted Tiger declined, saying that he and his family had already made plans for a long vacation. Privately, he wondered whether the president would have extended this offer had he not won. Well, everyone knows the answer to that one, including the ubiquitous Al Sharpton, who put an interesting spin on the situation some weeks later . He pointed out that America was quick to celebrate Tiger's multiracial heritage as soon as he won the Masters, and added that, had Tiger failed in his quest for the green jacket, he would simply have been the black kid who lost. There is more than a little irony to this view, and all too much truth.

Perhaps the best way to assess the impact of the events on April 13th, 1997, is to see what America is doing on April 13th, 2027. Hopefully, the nation will be celebrating something a lot more meaningful than golf's emergence from the dark ages.

It Don't Mean A Thing

The simplicity of the game of golf is, ultimately, what makes it so maddeningly complicated. On the surface, it is a small matter of dragging a bag from Point A to Point B. Yet each time a golfer draws back his club and sends it crashing into that dimpled sphere, his own mind, of all things, conspires to undo what years of study, practice, deep introspection and rational thinking have prepared him to accomplish. Thousands upon thousands of minute calculations must be made during the two seconds that it takes to draw back a golf club and send the ball on its way. Yet, if even a single one of those thoughts creeps into the conscious mind, you are dead. Of course, most golfers would die happy having strung a dozen or so good shots together just once in their lives.

For those who have yet to experience even this modest sliver of Nirvana, a young man like Tiger Woods is a source of both great wonder and sublime frustration. He seems to have it all figured out, as if he has played every shot there is to play—on every hole, on every course. Tiger hits long, he hits straight and he hits smart. And he hits with both daring and consistency. He is almost like a futuristic golfing cyborg, programmed since activation to execute perfect golf shots. He is that cool.

> *"Because we have so much speed, what would be a slight miss for most players becomes a real errant shot."*
> **Tiger, on the disadvantages of being among the PGA Tour's big hitters**

After watching Tiger swing, Arnold Palmer (left) and Jack Nicklaus predicted he would win more Masters than both of them combined.

Indeed, people can get carried away with how mature Tiger is, how polished he is for his age. But in the end, the why and how of his startling success are not that hard to figure out. Peel away the innocent smile, the youthful confidence and the very public baggage he has already begun to accumulate, and you get back to the thing that got him here, and the thing that will keep him here: the swing.

The speed of the club head is what astounds his fellow PGAers, and puts millions of television viewers on the edge of their seats. Tiger transfers energy from his body, through his arms and down the shaft of the club almost flawlessly. His backswing is smooth and relatively short, not even

*Golf manufacturers are already gearing up
to meet the demand for new clubs as a
result of Tiger's popularity.*

> *"Tiger generates the most efficient club-head-speed to ball-speed relationship...when you're able to keep the spin down and the launch up, it results in tee shots with very boring trajectory."*
> **Titleist president Wally Uihlein**

parallel to the ground. His grip is textbook, as is his posture. The tremendous force Tiger generates is created by a shoulder turn of around 120 degrees, with his hip turn limited to about 30. And then, in one explosive motion, he releases the power stored in his broad shoulders and powerful thighs, wrapping it around his wasp-thin 28-inch waist to connect with the ball at an estimated 200 miles per hour. At the same time, the club face is square, and the trajectory of the swing is as close to perfect as there is on the pro tour. Indeed, Titleist has been testing pros for two decades, measuring their combination of swing speed and angle of impact. Tiger comes closer to the ideal—a nine degree trajectory with a minimum of backswing—than anyone they ever tested. Other golfers may

generate similar club speed, but Tiger's ability to hit the ball perfectly makes him the longest driver on the PGA Tour. By a lot. As previously mentioned, although he fell short of the minimum number of rounds in 1996, his driving average in the 41 rounds he did play was the highest in PGA history.

To execute this swing requires a combination of strength, supreme physical coordination, and the ability to switch emotions over to auto-pilot for a couple of seconds. Every MPH added to the swing brings with it the potential for untold disaster, and when you swing that hard, any mental glitch, however microscopic, is amplified a thousandfold. That Tiger is able to send the ball sizzling off the tee—while attaining such remarkable distance and accuracy—provides

Tiger may be known for his 330-yard drives off the tee, but it is creativity with his irons that so impresses veteran pros.

is where Tiger has excelled from the moment he joined the professional tour. Where other golfers draw upon years of experience to negotiate their way around doglegs, Tiger just blasts the ball over the trees. From there, a short iron usually gets him to the greens, where his putting takes over. His already-superb short game continues to get better, and his putting goes from good to great when tournaments are on the line.

By the way, Tiger's swing gives him an advantage which may not be obvious to his growing legion of fans. Because most of the energy needed to propel a golf ball is generated by the *speed* of the club head, and not the *weight* of the club head, he can use a lighter club than most other pros. He favors a driver with a stainless steel head and steel shaft, not the titanium head and graphite shaft that has become so prevalent on the tour. And because a lighter club is far easier to control than a heavy one, Tiger is far less likely to lose the groove or get tired in the final round of an event.

irrefutable evidence that he possesses these qualities. That he has acquired his skills logging so few golf miles is what everyone finds most amazing.

Translating talent off the tees into tournament victories, however, can be a tricky business. But, of course, this

O h, and here's a frightening thought: Tiger is only swinging at 70 to 80 percent off the tee. In other words, he could hit the ball even farther if he wanted. The trick in golf, of course, is to remain consistent and accurate, and Tiger feels he can give away a little distance. If he needs a 360-yard bazooka shot, he can always squeeze one off. But in general, he concentrates on controlling his power more than maximizing it. In fact, his driver is 43 inches—an inch shorter than most pros use—and he uses a three-piece ball instead of the harder, longer-flying two-piece ball. And the guy still reaches the par fives in two.

So how long has Tiger been PGA-ready? Could he have mopped up the course with the likes of Couples and Love had he joined the tour in '95? Or even earlier? Definitely not. The golf world has been hearing Tiger's name for years now, so it is only natural to assume that his game has been on this high plane since some time shortly after infancy. The truth is that, although he has distinguished himself at every level, his explosive swing might have been his undoing had he turned pro much before he did.

Though still just a baby by PGA standards, Tiger hits out of the sand as well as anyone on the tour.

Even when he was capturing all those amateur championships, Tiger had the kind of narrow stance and exaggerated backswing that robbed him of power and accuracy. He tried to make up for it with quick hands and footwork, and to his credit, it usually worked. But once or twice a round, Tiger would send a tee shot hissing into the trees, costing him precious strokes and, sometimes, tournaments. Not until he spread his stance out beyond the width of his shoulders—which produced less hip turn and shortened his swing—did the major flaws in Tiger's game begin to disappear. From there, it was a matter of making minor adjustments.

Among the most important was one he made prior to the '96 Amateur Championship. Tiger had always been taught to keep his right elbow close to his body when he started his backswing. But this was resulting in an overly steep swing, which kept him from maxing out his drives off the tee. Working with instructor Butch Harmon, Tiger found that he could let his elbow fly away from his body

and attain full extension without letting his wrists get too loose. That extension paid off when the club head came back down, and the results were some monster drives that helped him take the tournament. Another key to Tiger's swing is his shoulder turn. Like most young golfers, he tucked his left shoulder under his chin on the takeaway. But when he began taking it *past* his chin, he found he could shift his weight better to the right and achieve a more complete upper-body coil. Add another five to 10 yards to his distance off the tee.

Alas, there is something comforting in the knowledge that Tiger had to battle a few mechanical demons before he coolly dismantled the pro tour. It reaffirms his humanity, leaves room for (gulp) further improvement, and gives fans something to root for as everyone else tries to catch a little of that magic and keep up with young Mr. Woods.

> *"When I grow up, I want to have a swing as pretty as his."*
> **Jack Nicklaus, after watching Tiger at age 17**

> "He hits the ball a mile, he's got a brilliant short game, he can putt, and he has the imagination to make shots. It's the total package."
> **Mike Francesa, CBS commentator**

The more at stake, the better Tiger usually putts. He is not afraid to tinker with his stroke, as he did in the three tournaments prior to the 1997 Masters.

Into The Woods

Is the whole of Tiger Woods greater than the sum of his parts? When you start separating what he has accomplished from what he has become, do you get a better sense of what makes Tiger tick?

These are questions his fans are just beginning to ask, and it may be quite a while before the answers emerge. Until the big picture is clearer, everyone will simply have to be satisfied with a lot of little ones. But really, is that so bad? After all, sometimes the best way to appreciate a masterpiece is to examine the master's brushstrokes.

In the meantime, here are some Tiger tidbits to satisfy even the most voracious appetite...

- At 15, Tiger was the youngest player to win the U.S. Junior title.

- Tiger is the only three-time winner of the U.S. Junior championship, and he won each on the last hole.

Tiger played the U.S. Amateur three times before winning it in 1994. The first time he competed he was only 15.

- Tiger is the youngest golfer—and the first African-American—ever to win the U.S. Amateur Championship.

- Tiger is the only golfer to win the U.S. Amateur three consecutive times.

- In 1996, Tiger became the first PGA Tour player to average more than 300 yards off the tee after 30 rounds. He also became the youngest golfer ever to top the $1 million mark in tournament winnings.

- He is the only man to win the National Junior and Amateur titles, capturing each three times.

- Tiger and Bobby Jones are the only players ever to win USGA titles six years in a row.

"Obviously, golf is a very serious part of my life, but when you stop having fun at it, that's when it's time to hang it up."
Tiger

- Tiger's 18 straight match-play victories and .909 winning percentage are the best in the history of the U.S. Amateur Championship.

- Tiger's swing coach, Butch Harmon, charges $300 an hour for lessons. In 1948, Butch's dad—a club pro—shocked the world by winning the Masters.

Tiger's caddy at Augusta, Mike "Fluff" Cowan, said winning the Masters was almost as good as front-row seats at a Grateful Dead concert. Cowan's partnership with Tiger has made him the most recognizable caddy in America.

> *"This year I am experimenting. This is my first full year as a professional and I will see what I can handle. It is a learning process. I will just see what my body can take and what I can do. If my body cannot handle it, at least I will have learned."*
> **Tiger, on scheduling and traveling**

- After the 1996 season, Tiger rescheduled the Haskins Award dinner he had abruptly cancelled and gave one of the most heartfelt and sincere apologies anyone could remember. The attendees responded with a standing ovation.

- There are still more than 20 courses in the United States that Tiger can't play because his great grandfather was black.

- Tiger has started his own foundation, which will send sports psychologists into underprivileged neighborhoods to teach kids how to play golf, and increase their self worth.

- Tiger was a finalist for the 1996 Sullivan Award as the nation's top amateur athlete.

- Tiger, Jack Nicklaus and Phil Mickelson are the only players to win an NCAA and U.S. Amateur title the same year.

- After Tiger's Las Vegas win, Michael Jordan said his hero was Tiger Woods.

- Tiger maintained a solid B+/A- grade average throughout high school.

- Tiger never had a babysitter growing up, and he never had a job.

> *"Have I been lucky? No doubt. You have to get good breaks in order to win."*
> **Tiger**

- By the end of the 1996 season, Tiger set a PGA Tour record for lowest scoring average, and led the tour in driving average, birdies per round and eagle frequency.

- During his amazing run for a third consecutive U.S. Amateur title, Tiger replaced sports psychologist/caddie Jay Brunza—who had been at his side for all five of Tiger's previous USGA titles—with Byron Bell, his best friend since boyhood.

- Tiger studied economics at Stanford. He has promised his parents that he will one day complete his degree.

- When Tiger is asked to fill in the space for ethnicity on tournament applications, he usually writes "Asian".

- Before playing a tournament with fast greens, Tiger used to practice his putting on the kitchen floor. In college, he would use Stanford's Maples Pavilion basketball court.

- Although the Woods family has moved, Earl has not sold the home in Cypress. He would like to keep it as a Tiger museum, to inspire other kids.

- Tiger and Earl have a special way of communicating when they are separated by large crowds. They call each other "Sam".

- Within a week of Tiger's victory at Augusta, the PGA Tour began negotiating long-term deals with several broadcast and cable networks.

> *"I am the toughest golfer mentally."*
> **Tiger**

Tiger enjoys the boisterous galleries that follow him around the course.

- Tiger never modeled his game on any one golfer. Instead, he broke down the games of several top pros and borrowed what he thought was the best from each. He became a great mimic of golf's most distinctive swings, entertaining friends with imitations of Chi Chi Rodriguez, Lee Trevino, Greg Norman and Gary Player.

- Tiger understands the importance of maintaining a personal connection with his fans, no matter how big his gallery gets. After nailing his first professional hole-in-one at the Greater Milwaukee Open, he tossed the ball into the crowd. Tiger regularly gives away his golf balls while he's playing, and tries to sign autographs for up to an hour after each round.

- When torrential rain and gale-force winds pelted Northern California in 1994, Tiger went out to the golf course and knocked balls into the wind. He thought it would be a perfect way to practice for the British Open.

- Tiger and Earl give lively clinics to inner-city children, concentrating on anti-drug and stay-in-school messages.

- Tiger actually feeds off the energy of the gallery and acknowledges their support. Where other golfers would just as soon play on an empty course, Tiger's mental toughness actually turns a pulsating throng to his advantage.

- At Western High in Anaheim, Tiger excelled as a switch-hitter, pass catcher, shooting guard and sprinter, but decided to concentrate on golf.

- Tiger believes anger should be turned into creative energy. If someone does something to hurt you, just beat them, whatever their game.

- Tiger credits his fast start on the PGA Tour to his frame of mind heading into tournaments. Whereas most pros approach an event hoping to shoot between five and ten under par, Tiger goes in thinking about only one thing: winning.

"For some reason, I don't mind being down. It's no big deal because I know what I can do. It's just a matter of doing it."
Tiger

- When opponents put pressure on Tiger, he responds by hitting more aggressively, instead of freezing up. This makes him hard to hold off and almost impossible to catch. Through his play, Tiger tries to reflect pressure back on his opponents.

> *"Golf is basically a vehicle for me to help people...I can touch people, I can inspire lives in a positive way."*
> **Tiger**

- Tiger teamed with Kelli Kuehne, whose brother Trip he defeated for his first U.S. Amateur title, at the 1997 JCPenney Classic.

> *"I've learned to trust the subconscious. My instincts have never lied to me."*
>
> **Tiger on how he makes some of his more outrageous shots**

- Tiger wears contact lenses during the day, but often switches to glasses in the evenings. His Stanford teammates used to tease him, calling him Urkel because of how he looked in specs.

- After winning the Honda Classic in Thailand, Tiger was made an honorary Thai citizen.

- How does Tiger feel about the golf world's great expectations? He claims they don't bother him, because they will never exceed his own.

- When Tiger gets frustrated by a sub-par round, he does whatever he has to in order to blow off steam and then moves on. After falling short at the 1996 Texas Open by a couple of missed putts, Tiger slammed the door to his hotel room and broke eight putters over his knee. Then he calmly analyzed his performance.

> *"So far I've been able to perform when it counts."*
>
> **Tiger**

Tiger's trip to Thailand included meeting Prime Minister Chaowalit Yongchaiyudh, and being made an honorary citizen of the country where his mother was born.

A picture may be worth a thousand words most places, but among the members of the golfing fraternity words of praise are like hen's teeth. That's why golfers just don't get very excited when they see a hot, young player because, frankly, they've seen too many crash and burn. Even if they have an inkling that a newcomer has a bright future ahead of him, they generally keep that kind of insight to themselves. This has not been the case since Tiger Woods arrived on the scene. The accolades have been heaped upon him since he was knee-high to a sand wedge, and they have grown louder, more effusive and more sincere each time he has put another notch in his belt. How good is Tiger? How much better can he be? Take a look at what these folks have to say on the subject...

> "By the time he's 30... I can see interest doubling, tripling, quadrupling."
>
> **John Merchant,**
> **CEO National Minority**
> **Golf Association**

"How great will his career be? If things go right, Tiger will win twelve majors and 50 tournaments, which is comparable to Jack Nicklaus' record, considering the improved level of competition Tiger will see over his career. He'll also be as popular as Arnold Palmer in his prime."

Johnny Miller

> "I think he's the kind of young man who will play the game of golf for the game of golf."
> **Jack Nicklaus**

*"Tiger has that competitive meanness.
When he's on the course, he will tear your
head off and spit down your neck."*
Curtis Strange

"He has all the elements to be a superstar—in the world, not just in golf. Tiger is young, he's nice looking, he's charismatic. There is something there that's enough to make people say, 'We're going to follow this kid.'"

Joyce Julius, Sports Marketing Expert

"He's got genetics that other players don't have. He's got a sound golf swing. His fundamentals are good. He's got great strength, speed and hand-eye coordination. Combine all that and it produces that almighty smack."

David Leadbetter, Teaching Pro

> "I wouldn't care if he became a plumber."
>
> **Earl, the day Tiger turned pro**

> "He would be a world-class 400-meter runner and kicking Michael Johnson's ass. If you think Tiger's swing is pretty, you should see him run."
>
> **Earl, on what Tiger would be doing if he didn't play golf**

> "Tiger Woods, like Michael Jordan, cuts across ethnic groups and age groups. He just transcends all of those things."
>
> **Nike CEO Phillip Knight**

"He's the intimidator."

Fred Couples

"He's probably the best player that I have ever seen."

Raymond Floyd

"Tiger is the prototypical golfer for the 21st century. He's the person Jack Nicklaus said would come along and replace him. He hits long, hits straight, has great touch and is a good athlete... he doesn't have a real weakness."

Instructor Jack Cook

"I've never seen anyone come onto the scene with as much publicity, and outperform it."

Jack Nicklaus

"His heart, his sense of occasion—is as strong as anybody's I've ever seen."

Chuck Cook, Teaching Pro

"He handles himself like a gentleman, like a champion, almost like a king."

Mike Francesa, sports commentator

"He's the most important young golfer in the last 50 years."

Tom Watson

"Tiger is better at his age than anybody that's ever been...if he continues to maintain his game, he will be the best player ever."
Byron Nelson

"He'd rather golf than eat, and he's a professional eater. He'd rather golf than sleep, and he's a professional sleeper."
Earl Woods

"We need him. Golf needs more good young players. The thing is, too, he's a nice guy."
Andy North

"He's just in another stratosphere...the kid is just so amazing. I have total admiration for him."

Jim Nantz, CBS golf commentator

"Tiger is playing a much simpler game."

Scott Simpson

"He's like a sponge. He just soaks up knowledge like it's going out of style."

Butch Harmon, Tiger's coach since 1993

"Someday there will be a dominant player who wins two majors and eight tournaments in a year. Maybe it'll be Tiger, or somebody motivated by Tiger."

Tom Lehman

"He has everything...the power...the know how...and the shot-making ability. "
Lee Trevino

"In an era of boastful, loud-mouthed, look-at-me superstars, this young man is thoughtful, polite and soft-spoken."

National Columnist, Stedman Graham

"He transcends golf."

Titleist President Wally Uihlein

"Tiger is a great kid. He's carried himself like a true champion."

Charlie Sifford

Winning Colors
A Word About Political Correctness

If one could peer into a crystal ball and get a glimpse of life in the 21st century, it seems fairly certain that one would find this country less divided along racial lines, if only because those lines are likely to become more and more obscured. The American melting pot, which once fused all nationalities into one, is now doing the same for the different races. And as Tiger reminds us all, what you think you see is not always what you get.

All Tiger Woods wants to be is a champion. But as he has discovered, it is not that simple. Blacks want a black champion. Asians want an Asian champion. And Native Americans want a Native American champion. And a lot of people don't want him to be a champion at all. From his earliest years on the golf course, Tiger could feel the disapproving eyes upon him. And ever since then, with all of the hate mail, death threats, snubs and snide remarks, he has never forgotten that as good as he is with a club in his hands, as a golfer of color he will always be fighting an uphill battle.

It is a battle for which Earl trained him well. Tiger has heard many times his father's stories of the racism he encountered in college and the army. And from his father, he first learned about barrier breakers like Jackie Robinson, as well as great black golfers, including Teddy Rhodes, Charlie Owens, Charlie Sifford, Calvin Peete and Lee Elder. But being black is not what Tiger is all about. Yes, he recognizes that as far as America is concerned, that it the category into

> *"He's going to to do something I always wanted to do but never really had the opportunity to: he's going to win a lot. And when he does, there's going to be kids who notice it, and think about playing."*
> **Charlie Sifford**

Golfer Ted Rhodes was the first African-American to play in a PGA-sanctioned event. Rhodes passed away in 1969.

which he most conveniently fits. However, mathematically speaking, he is more Asian than black—a fact his mother never tires of pointing out.

Most all of the ill will directed toward Tiger thus far has been anti-black. From the day he was tied to a tree and taunted in kindergarten, to the comments made in jest by Fuzzy Zoeller after he won the 1997 Masters, it has been the color of his skin that has drawn the most attention. There was the anonymous note he received after his first Masters, which said, "Just what we don't need, another nigger in sports." And the letter he opened as a freshman at Stanford, which read, "You can take the nigger

Lee Elder broke the color barrier at the Masters in 1975. He flew into Augusta to be on hand for Tiger's tremendous victory.

Ultimately, whatever Tiger achieves he will achieve for the human race, including Africans, Europeans, Asians, Native Americans and even those whose blood does not course through his veins. Not that he harbors any illusions about this being a perfect planet, but you have to start somewhere. In that respect, Tiger will

out of the jungle, but you can't take the jungle out of the nigger." He taped that one to the wall of his dorm room, just as he had the motivational messages and Jack Nicklaus's record in his room back home. They are all additives in the fuel that powers him. In fact, IMG now has instructions to save any hate mail Tiger receives and pass it along to him, just in case he ever starts feeling as if he has the world licked.

> *"Why me? Why so late? It's kind of sad. It should have started with Charlie Owens, Teddy Rhodes, Calvin Peete—all these other blacks who came before me. It should have happened in the 1950s. But prejudice still reigned, I think, and it's kind of sad."*
> **Tiger**

> ## *"Growing up, I came up with this name: I'm a Cablinasian."*
> **Tiger, on his Caucasian-Black-Indian-Asian racial mix**

continue to identify himself as "multiracial" at every opportunity, and he will continue to hope that in some small way his deeds will soften the division between the white world and his own. At the very least, Tiger will help focus attention on the growing issue of multiracialism in this country, which promises to be one of the more profound social forces that will help to shape this country during Tiger's lifetime.

Calvin Peete won the Greater Milwaukee Open twice in his career, and in 1983 led the PGA in driving accuracy and greens in regulation. In '84, Peete edged Jack Nicklaus for the Vardon Trophy with the tour's lowest scoring average.

The 19th Hole

We sportswriters have to be careful with a guy like Tiger Woods. So much of our lives is dedicated to putting a socially significant spin on runs, hits and errors that when a bona fide socially significant individual actually does come along, we run the risk of turning into blithering idiots, stating and restating the obvious, blurting out whatever comes to mind, just to be the first person to say something that no one else has said yet. Truth be told, not enough of the Tiger Woods story has unfolded to even begin making the kind of blanket statements one already sees in the press on a daily basis. Any meaningful evaluation of Tiger's ultimate importance, impact, et cetera, will have to wait for a few years. Or perhaps even a few decades. Rome was not built in a day, remember.

For now, the safest, smartest way to size up Tiger and how he fits into the big picture is to keep any observations and opinions grounded in the world of golf. Certainly, that is Tiger's plan. He knows that if he does not continue playing on a high level, all the other stuff will seem like a big joke. Yes, Tiger could one day have a lasting impact on society, but if he loses his focuses on the links, he will not be the Jackie Robinson of golf, but the Willie O'Ree, whom you will need to look up in your Hockey Encyclopedia.

So if one sticks to golf, and also recognizes that these are still the formative stages of Tiger's career, what are the most interesting and important things to notice about Mr. Woods?

If Tiger has his way, fewer kids will be on the outside of golf looking in.

Now more than ever, Tiger needs to stay focused on golf. If he doesn't keep winning, his long-term impact on the sport might be greatly diminished.

The first, the most obvious, and potentially the most devilishly funny, is that thanks to Tiger the PGA Tour must start grappling with something that heretofore has been little more than a vague, misty concept for the guys in the plaid pants: political correctness. Tiger, unlike the game's earlier black pioneers, is going to be generating a lot of cash for golf. And that cash will undoubtedly trickle down into the pockets of anyone who cares to get with the plan. This means that the PGA's players, staffers and officials must develop an awareness and understanding of people who are different, less fortunate and not nearly as privileged.

> *"You take your bumps, you take your licks, and you get up and shake them off and you keep on ticking and moving forward."*
> **Fuzzy Zoeller, on the fallout from his comments on Tiger**

One measure of Tiger's fame is that more people now know Fuzzy Zoeller's name than ever before.

Pigs will fly, hell will freeze over and we may even see another Polish Pope before that level of enlightenment comes to pass. In the meantime, we can watch with glee as everyone tries their best to seem like they have always been big-hearted, open-minded and color blind.

The first stab at welcoming Tiger to the club was made by Fuzzy Zoeller.

It was not a success. Indeed, however the PGA evolves in terms of political correctness, and whatever weird and winding road it takes in its odyssey from intolerance to acceptance, it will forever be divided into two distinct periods: *BT* (before Tiger) and *AZ* (after Zoeller). Fuzzy's words, and the strangely magnanimous way in which he uttered them, served as an example of just how far Tiger's peers had not come since he joined the tour in '96. For the record, Zoeller referred to Tiger as "that little boy," and suggested to reporters that they "pat him on the back, and say congratulations and enjoy it, and tell him not to serve fried chicken next year [at the Masters dinner, for which Tiger gets to pick the menu]. Or collard greens or whatever the hell they serve."

In the bizarre wake of this incident, K-Mart may have lost an endorsing athlete, but the tour gained what it desperately needed to take that first giant step out of the 19th century and into the 21st: it had a convenient and well-deserving fall guy. If Tiger was golf's second coming, then why not just make Fuzzy golf's Pontius Pilate? Imagine the great good luck to have

Zoeller out there making an ass of himself within moments of Tiger slipping on the green jacket. Amazing. Instead of banging out editorials on how Augusta would now have to deal with past sins, or how golf was on the verge of becoming an everyman's game, the feature writers, columnists, and talking heads could just pound on Fuzzy.

Did Tiger play the situation smart? As smart as could be expected of a 21-year-old. He let Fuzzy swing in the

> *"Athletes aren't as gentlemanly as they used to be. I don't like that change. I like the idea of being a role model. It's an honor. People took the time to help me as a kid, and they impacted my life. I want to do the same for kids."*
> **Tiger, on his off-the-course responsibilities.**

wind for a couple of days, then carefully forgave what he said but not why he said it. Having himself been sandbagged by a reporter from *GQ*, who printed several off-color jokes about black stereotypes that Tiger believed were off the record, he knew that he could have been accused, just as easily as Zoeller, of making insensitive and stupid remarks about blacks. Tiger knew Fuzzy meant no

> *"What's appropriate in America anymore? What I said at Augusta was kind of a joke, and I got nailed for it."*
> **Fuzzy Zoeller**

harm, but he rightly took exception to the thinking behind the remarks; Zoeller was asked to comment on a talented and complex young man and could not get beyond his complexion. Tiger knows he can never extinguish that kind of smoldering bigotry. But he has served notice on his PGA brethren that, in no uncertain terms, the party is over. Tiger and the new

army of golf fans he is bringing to the sport will be watching and listening carefully for any actions or words that even hint at racial prejudice. The pendulum has swung from the old all-caucasian rule to the no-more-black-Asian-Indian jokes rule. Let's see, that leaves what? Political satire?

In some ways, it was a shame that Fuzzy Zoeller had to be the one who will forever serve as a monument to everything Tiger must overcome. By all accounts, he is one of the many decent, normal guys on the tour, and he is as close to an intellectual as one is likely to find in pro golf. In fact, he was long considered by his peers to be something of a wit. As it turned out, they were half right. Welcome to the world of golf, everyone. And welcome to reality, Fuzzy.

So now that everyone is on his best behavior, the gaffes should get even better. Don't think for a moment that some of the golf establishment won't reveal its old self. This should make for both high drama and high comedy, and golf fans old and new should just sit back and enjoy it, for however painful this process is, it should ultimately yield positive results.

There is another aspect of Tiger Woods that may also foreshadow something of a new era in sports. Tiger is, and always has been, a video game freak. Predictably, he favors the one-on-one fighting games, where a few carefully placed blows with a medieval weapon (a club, perhaps?) send streams of blood gushing from an opponent's gaping wounds. Tiger grew up on this stuff, as have millions of American kids. In fact, video games are a new and perhaps significant element in the makeup of the current generation of 20-somethings, especially as they relate to athletics. There is a fearlessness borne of the "reset" button, which allows a kid to spring back to life regardless of how badly burned, bludgeoned or hacked to bits he is. Dying, therefore, carries no consequences. By the same token, in-your-face aggressiveness and mindless, sustained ferocity are rewarded. The combination makes for some pretty wired kids. This is not the mind-numbing simplicity of Pong, mind you, nor the mundane Cold War paranoia of Space Invaders. The video games that have been coming down the pike during the past

> *"We are expecting nothing but the best words, the best actions, the best shots. Everything has to be the best from Tiger Woods. That's sad, because I think we are all entitled to mistakes... He's still a young man. Let's let him grow and naturally develop... Let's give the man a chance to establish his own identity, and establish his own success."*
> **Hale Irwin**

half-decade are pretty damn realistic and stunningly graphic in their depiction of violence. And, you guessed it, Tiger Woods turns to these games for *relaxation*.

The way these games are played is important to understand, too. The best video jockeys—and by all accounts Tiger is one—work on every nuance of a particular game until they feel they can react appropriately to any situation. They know instinctively when it is time to advance, and when it is best to retreat. They know when to play something by the book, and when to improvise. There is no time for fear, self-analysis or self-doubt. Once they have played a game a few hundred times, they slip into a semi-conscious state of intense concentration, where mind and body truly work as one and everything else is shut out. They get totally locked in, for an hour or two a day, six or seven days a week, often for an entire adolescence. In other words, these kids spend more time in "the zone" on a typical day than Michael Jordan or Andre Agassi do in a typical month. Yet as much improvisation as a video game demands, it is still a computer program, which means in the long run a great player must have, above all else, tremendous consistency and discipline. Is this beginning to sound familiar?

Will Tiger's video game skills herald a new age for golf?

In addition to the mental coolness of a trained killer, a graduate of the video game wars has an interesting physical attribute: the ability to make super-fine adjustments, on the fly, with the wrist, hand and fingers. The line between living and dying in a video game can be as subtle as a well-timed muscle twitch with the fourth finger. Essentially, the new video games have produced a teenage army of cold, calculated killers with ultrafine muscle control. Now whether this is America's great untapped resource is definitely open to debate—by and large, these kids have only a passing interest in physical activity, and their needle barely registers on the ambition scale. But couple these unusual qualities with an athlete's body and training, and suddenly you have a rather intriguing proposition.

Think of the sports where these video-bred advantages might give a player an edge. Certainly, in a game such as tennis, where a flick of the wrist can produce a sparkling winner and a split-second lapse in concentration can cost a crucial point, the combination of dexterity and extreme tunnel-vision would prove a great advantage. Or in baseball, where a batter must read and react to a pitch in two tenths of a second, and a hurler must make delicate adjustments to his delivery to make the ball go where, and do as, he pleases. But of all the sports that might welcome such added skills, golf would seem to stand alone as the perfect medium for the video game generation. It rewards both the ability to repeat complex maneuvers and to make minute adjustments. Golf demands intense focus, but also requires problem-solving skills. And when golfers step up to the ball, they must be able to slam their minds shut on everything around them and simply concentrate on making the shot. Sounding even more familiar?

Like all touring pros, Tiger gets upset with himself when he makes a mistake. The challenges he will be facing off the course may leave him even less margin for error.

Consider what happens now when someone like Tom Kite finds himself a few strokes up with nine holes to play. His lead is relatively safe, because the guy chasing him is feeling the pressure, worrying what will happen if he becomes too aggressive, and doubting deep down if he is even capable of catching one of golf's great players. Now take Kite's pursuer, dump in a video-game brain, and suddenly you have a very interesting situation. This person has dispatched thousands of 16-bit enemies in hand-to-hand combat, and has himself been killed so many times that the idea of failure—even on its most profound level—is not even a consideration anymore. This cyber golfer, or whatever one chooses to call him, is not worried about the public embarrassment of blowing risky shots, because to him failure has always been an anonymous experience. In fact, it is simply a way of learning how to get better when you play the game again. If he screws up, if he dies, so what? Game over. He can push the reset button and start all over again from zero on Thursday when the next tournament rolls around.

Granted, on one level, this idea of a video-game-bred generation of golfers, led by Tiger Woods, might seem silly and trivial. Then again, doesn't every generation bring something new and unique to the sport? The cold-blooded, ultracompetitive cyber golfer is something the PGA Tour has never really experienced before, and who knows, maybe all the young guys coming up behind Tiger will use this to great advantage, too. A player who can discard all the psychological baggage that makes the game so difficult, and just try to get the best score possible, makes for a formidable opponent. He is playing against the course, playing against himself, and playing to beat his own high score. The hell with the crowds, the other golfers, the protocol and the tradition. The idea is to win. This is the world of Tiger Woods, the first athlete to add video game skills to his arsenal. And chances are, he will not be the last.

Away from the PGA Tour, Tiger's long-term impact, as mentioned, is impossible to predict. Can one glean anything thus far? Well, he has had a short-term effect on our society, especially since winning the Masters. Tiger has rank-and-file America doing some deep thinking about three things, two of which are actually important: kids, race and golf.

Contrary to popular belief, the emerging generation—Post-Gen-X, if you will—has much to offer as we close out America's second full century and move toward what, with any luck, will be its third. Born in the disco era, suckled on the Reagan years and schooled during a decade of global uncertainty, the kids coming out of their teens are in many ways primed to make their mark on society even as baby boomers seek to secure their twilight years in the coming decades. They are comfortable with emerging technologies (more inclined to work for and with them than against them) and less hung-up on race, religion and politics than their predecessors. They see the world as a shrinking entity, not

Tiger's incredible start on the PGA Tour has made him one of the most recognized athletes in the world. Today he is on a par with (from left) Monica Seles, Andre Agassi, Shaquille O'Neal and Ken Griffey, Jr. Will he soon surpass them in popularity?

a yawning void; they sense that what today is out of their control is likely tomorrow to be within their grasp. It may not yet be an article of faith, but it is a fine foundation for the future. Tiger might not end up as his generation's poster boy—er, person—but like Tiger, his generation is primed to carve out a high-profile place in 21st century society.

Where race is concerned, Tiger could well prove to be a poster person, for unlike age, ethnic makeup never changes. Consider this: By the time Tiger takes his last swing as a touring pro, the United States will probably be less than half white. And less than half black. That means Tiger will look like most Americans, or if you prefer, vice versa. Hopefully, between today and that day in the far-off future, he will keep that issue in the headlines, so that one day it is less an issue than, say, class or gender. His is the face of the future, and it is high time everyone get used to it.

Relative to the social issues Tiger has brought to the fore, golf would seem at first glance to be little more than an afterthought. But remember, golf is what put Tiger in the spotlight

> **"It's amazing how everyone becomes an expert on my life."**
> **Tiger on all the advice he has received since turning pro**

and it is what will keep him there. If more minorities play the game, that would be great. If more parents steer their kids in that direction, that would be great, too. Clearly, Tiger possesses all of the qualities that enable a single athlete to take a sport from cult status to a national phenomenon.

But for Tiger to truly matter—for him to actually change the world, as his parents insist he will—he does need to stay at the very top of his game. That may not be easy, given what has been thrust upon Tiger, and the added weight he will be asked to bear between tournaments. Earl may have prepared him to hit long and true when keys are jangled and golf bags are dropped, but could Tiger possibly be prepared to pull off the three-way balancing act between athlete, corporate entity and symbol of hope and good that he is already being asked to perform? And if by some miracle he is, does he really want to? Even the manic plate-spinner who used to thrill audiences on the old *Ed Sullivan Show* cracked a dish or two. If he assumes this impossible role, Tiger may not have that luxury.

Reason tells us that, in the end, he—and we—shall find a comfortable middle ground. Tiger cannot continue being everything to everyone and anything to anyone. If he tries, he will lose his youth and maybe even his humanity. Already mature beyond his years, he will gain even more wisdom as he moves between worlds, and eventually hit on a solution every bit as unique and clever as Tiger himself. Until then, the Tiger Woods story should continue to be one of the most compelling sagas of celebrity and achievement in the annals of sports. And that should be good enough, whatever one's agenda and wherever one's loyalties lie.

> *"There are a lot of Tiger Woodses out there, if they were just given the opportunity to play. So many times black families don't have enough money to put the right equipment in their kids' hands."*
> **Earl Woods**

Wherever the next few years lead Tiger, connecting with kids will always remain a top priority.

About the Author

Mark Stewart

Mark Stewart ranks among the most prolific sportswriters of the 1990s. He has produced hundreds of profiles on athletes past and present, and authored more than 40 books, including biographies of Jeff Gordon, Monica Seles, Steve Young, Hakeem Olajuwan and Cecil Fielder. A graduate of Duke University, Stewart has served as senior editor of *Racquet Magazine*, a national tennis magazine, and *Super News*, a sporting goods industry newspaper. His first books—*The Ultimate Insider's Guide to Baseball Cards* and *Nick Bollettieri's Five Keys to Tennis*—were published in 1992. He is currently president of Team Stewart, Inc., a sports information and resource company located in Monmouth County, New Jersey.

Credits / Dedication

PHOTO CREDITS

All photos courtesy AP/Wide World Photos, Inc. except the following:

Rusty Jarrett./AllSport – page 29
Alan D. Levenson/AllSport – page 14
Ken Levine/AllSport – page 20
Gary Newkirk/AllSport – page 23, page 26

STAFF

Executive Producers:
Fred Sammis and John Bergin

Project Coordinator:
John Sammis
Cronopio Publishing

Design and Electronic Page Makeup:
 Ron Jaffe
Jaffe Enterprises

DEDICATION

For Rachel, Mariah & Sarah
Mark Stewart